A FUNNY WAY OF LIFE

THE KRANKIES: A 'FAN-DABI-DOZI'
AUTOBIOGRAPHY

IAN & JANETTE TOUGH WITH MATT
BENDORIS

Comedy duo Ian and Janette Tough became household names as The Krankies after performing in front of the Queen Mum and a television audience of millions at the Royal Variety Performance in 1978. With Janette portraying cheeky schoolboy Wee Jimmy Krankie and Ian as the exasperated adult trying to keep a lid on Jimmy's antics, they went on to revive the BBC1 institute Crackerjack! Before fronting their own popular shows including The Krankies Elektronik Komic, making them one of the biggest acts of the 1980s.

Their incredible career went on to span six decades, but now, in their own words, 'A Funny Way Of Life' provides one of the most surprising, intriguing and downright fun autobiographies you will ever read.

Copyright © Ian and Janette Tough (The Krankies) and Matt Bendoris 2004 and 2024.

All rights reserved. No part of this publication may be produced, stored in a retrieval system, or transmitted, in any form or by any means, electronic, mechanical, photocopying, recording or otherwise, without first obtaining written permission from the copyright owner.

A BAAM Books paperback edition

Cover design Smith Design Solutions Ltd

Front cover image: © Ian and Janette Tough (The Krankies)

Back cover image: © Wattie Cheung

For all the staff at Brinsworth House retirement home for entertainers

INTRODUCTION

HUSBAND and wife team Ian and Janette Tough became one of Britain's best loved comedy duos as The Krankies - rocketing to fame at the Royal Variety Performance where they delighted the Queen Mum and a television audience of millions in 1978.

Almost 11 years on national primetime TV was to follow as they went on to present - and revive - the failing BBC1 institution Crackerjack!, captivating and infuriating a nation in equal measures with their catchphrase 'Fan-Dabi-Dozi'.

Like Morecombe and Wise before them, they were then poached by the BBC's rivals ITV, to headline their Saturday evening line-up.

After three seasons the BBC decided they needed The Krankies back, and so in 1987 made them an offer they couldn't refuse.

But the times were-a-changin' and by the early 1990s attitudes towards The Krankies had changed in the TV corridors of power, where their act was now deemed to be 'seedy'.

The Krankies had had it rough before, but after so much success, this time it was even harder to take.

But they dusted themselves down and continued to do

panto, started working the Cruise Ship circuits, toured Australia during our harsh winter months every year and played a lot of golf.

By the end of the 1990s, after nearly 10 years away from TV, their fortunes began to change for the better as they earned the coveted 'cult status' thanks to hilarious appearances on hit comedy shows including French & Saunders (this time sending themselves up), regularly featured in Viz Magazine, and Janette also starred alongside Oscar-winner Julie Walters in the BBC series Dinner Ladies and in the 2003 series of Absolutely Fabulous.

The cameras also followed them once again for the documentary series The Real Marigold Hotel while they became regulars on the chat show circuit, appearing on Frank Skinner and Jonathan Ross's programmes where they would, as usual, be relentlessly quizzed about their 'curious' relationship.

Now in their autobiography, first released in 2004 and now updated 20 years on in 2024, they reveal in their own words the truth about their remarkable career and their marriage.

1

IAN'S STORY

I was born Ian Robert Tough on March 26, 1947, the middle child of three sons (My big brother Alistair is two years older than me and Colin 13 years my junior) into quite a privileged family of Clydebank Butchers, being delivered into the world at a private nursing home in Glasgow's Great Western Road. The family business had been started by my grandfather Robert, whose slogan was 'If it's Tough's - it's tender', before it was taken over by my dad Alex.

My mother Betty was from Manchester. She moved to Glasgow and met my dad who worked in the butchers by day and was also a football player for Ayr Utd at the time, playing outside left. We were better off than a lot of people at the time because it turned out my father had actually won £14,000 on the football pools in 1947, which is the equivalent of nearly £700,000 today. I never knew that until years later but it explained why we had a better house - a smart bungalow at 56 Drumry Road - and why we were born in private hospitals and always had new cars.

I was very ill when I was born with a condition that 16 years later would change the course of my life. I had lumps growing under my skin and spent the first six months in the Sick Children's Hospital. No one knew what was wrong with me. They thought it was some sort of blood disorder and put me on a new drug called penicillin and it seemed to cure me.

But when I was 16 I became very ill and nearly died. The surgeons removed my spleen as they discovered I had a diversion in my blood system - basically my blood was coursing around my body the wrong way. That is the defining moment that actually got me into show business because at the time I was an apprentice electrician and I couldn't do the heavy work after I left the hospital.

At school I had been an average student. I was intelligent enough but I hated every minute of it. I attended Radnor Park which ended up being condemned as they still had a bomb crater in the middle of the playground from the Clydebank Blitz, so we were moved to Kilbowie and then Braidfield Secondary.

I was a wild boy. I was actually hyperactive. Or ADHD they'd call it now. I remember when I was four I'd been so bad that for punishment my dad stripped me down to my underpants and put me in the butcher shop's window. When I was nine I smashed 10 windows in a local catholic school and broke four St Mary's statues and got caught red handed. I also bit the man who caught me. My dad was actually the local magistrate. There were no Children's Panels back then for me to be hauled in front of, and I was too young to be charged, so I'd get walloped by my dad, practically every night, but it made no difference whatsoever.

At ten I was caught putting rubber car tyres on the railway line - basically I was trying to derail a train, then I burnt down my garden shed. My parents didn't even need to ask, they knew it was me.

But surprisingly I could always make them laugh. They had to laugh or they'd cry. It was a case of 'oh no what's he done now?' The laughter probably saved their sanity. I honestly never set out to do bad things. I just didn't think. Not once, I just did it.

I was raised as a Protestant and I was made aware when I went to Kilbowie Church every Sunday that I wasn't supposed to have catholic friends. That's how backwards it was then - still is sadly in parts of Glasgow. It was very strange when Janette and I moved to England years later when we discovered people weren't bothered what faith you were born into. I liked that.

During my tearaway years I had an aunt Grace - a maiden aunt who never married - who was worried sick about me and told my parents I was hyperactive. She was an actress in the Clydebank Rep so she took me down to acting school. That's where I met Barbara Rafferty for the first time, who went on to find fame as Ella Cotter, in Rab C. Nesbitt. We were in a play together. I also met James Cosmo, who would star as Mel Gibson's sidekick in Braveheart and a host of other movies and TV shows. He even won Celebrity Big Brother. He was younger than me but was always a big, tall bugger and towered above the rest of us. Even then he was really ambitious, as he'd tell us he was going to be a big actor, and he certainly became a big actor in more ways than one and good luck to him.

I loved acting primarily because I was showing off. I never had any nerves or stage fright or anything like that. I would just get out there and everyone paid attention to me - perfect. My drama group took me to the Alhambra Theatre in Glasgow every Saturday. I loved being inside a real theatre. I'll never forget how excited I'd be at the weekend, knowing I was going there.

Although I found an outlet on stage, I never lost that nasty streak, which stayed with me right through to adulthood. As a young man I always tended to be a bit quick with my fists, especially if someone insulted Janette for her height. I remember in Sheffield we were walking down the street when someone shouted something like 'look at that short arse' - I just went for him. Janette hated that and she actually warned me if I did that again she was leaving me, because she couldn't stand it any longer.

It was the same when I was younger, I would actually batter guys older than me if they tried to pick on my big brother, I would nearly kill them. Alistair was a bookworm so others would have a go, but not if I was around.

When I went to the Theatre Guild at 14, that was the first time in my life that I acknowledged there were gay people in the world. This one gay guy, Robert Love, who was also in the guild, had said to my dad that he would keep an eye on me and nothing would happen - he was true to his word, everyone was nothing but nice to me. At this point I had left school and was doing an apprenticeship at James Scott and Company.

I had walked out of school because I was constantly beaten at Braidfield with a strap. They'd belt me for everything, I'd get walloped if I walked two paces faster than the art teacher on the way to class. When I look back on it I'm sure they were picking on me. Every bloody day. I just could not resist cheeking them back, then of course the rest of the class would piss themselves laughing and that just made me worse. So it was worth the pain. But when I'd go home my dad - who was an army man and a strict disciplinarian - would check if I had any marks on my wrists and if I did he'd belt me too. So basically I was belted constantly at home and at school. Today they'd be jailed, but that's just the way it was back then.

So when I left school at 15, the only qualification I had was a certificate in cycling proficiency - no kidding.

At James Scott and Company in Finnieston I worked as a store boy. I left school at Easter time and had to get up at six in the morning for work. Just two hours into my first day on the job I realised what a bloody mistake I'd made. It was hard work. The gaffers in there were worse than the school teachers -

much more frightening. They were big rough men, who'd belt you around the ear and make you do stupid things - all the usual stuff apprentices had to go through, like go and find me a left handed screwdriver and all that rubbish. Over the months though I gradually got to like it and these rough bastards got to like me. But when I was 16, after a day on a building site in Knightswood, I took ill when I got home that night. I was always an anaemic looking kid and dead skinny, not stocky like I am now. I had blood tests and something came up. The doctors kept asking if I'd ever been to Africa because I had all the symptoms of Yellow Fever - but I hadn't been out of Clydebank, never mind Scotland. Then they thought it may be blood cancer before discovering I had an enlarged spleen, which they decided to remove. I probably aggravated things as I was doing heavy work that day, cycled home, cut the lawn and drunk two bottles of fizzy drink which was about the worst thing I could have done. I was sick on the spot and spewed up blood. I was rushed into the Western Infirmary where they called for the minister because they thought I wasn't going to make it. I have a rare blood group, type B rhesus negative, but fortunately my brother Alistair has the same type so he was hooked up to give me a few pints. That probably saved me. Years later I was told that I was born a blue baby which meant I should have had a total blood transfusion at birth, but they had missed it, or just hadn't known in 1947.

I was in hospital for 16 weeks until they stopped the bleeding in my stomach. They actually put a balloon down my stomach and inflated it to stop the haemorrhaging. It worked. The blood was going the wrong way and was contaminating itself with toxins. So I still wasn't out of the woods because I caught pneumonia three times after that. But the doctors told me that I couldn't go back to heavy lifting again. James Scott were very good to me and said they'd retrain me as an electrician and would give me lighter work and I wouldn't have to go out on the building sites. In the meantime I was back in amateur dramatics and did Guys and Dolls at the Pavilion Theatre when I was 17 playing Liver Lips Louie.

The electrical manager at the Pavilion was always pissed and the stage manager Ian Gillespie kept saying that he would have to get rid of him. Being a chancer I told Ian that I could do that job. I was desperate to get into the theatre permanently. At the time I was fitting ships down on the dockyards and seeing guys who looked 60 but were only in their 40s. They'd be out in the worst weather with their welding gear, freezing their bollocks off in the snow and I just couldn't wait to get to the Pavilion when work finished. I loved the buzz of the theatre. I liked the people, there were all sorts, gay, straight, bi-sexual, but they were all softer people. They'd talk about The Stage newspaper and it was a completely different world which I longed to be a part of. So I started off as the light boy, then this old electrician got so bad that he was constantly steaming at work, that they finally got rid of him. The proprietor asked me if I could do the job of chief electrician and I bluffed it and said that I had my City and Guilds qualifications, which was nonsense. I didn't dare tell my dad that I had chucked James Scott for two weeks after I left. I would still get up at six o'clock and pretend I was going to work and would sit in a café in Glasgow's George Square until the theatre opened at 10am. I thought I was on easy street until the manager Mr Docherty informed me one day that Mr Balantyne, the proprietor wanted, to rewire the entire theatre and wished to know if his new Chief Electrician - i.e. ME - could have it done by. I was to start with the backstage area which was a complete mess. However, it just so happened that I had made friends with the foreman at an electrical company in Sauchiehall Street. I rushed up to him and said 'I'm really in the shit here, they want the Pavilion rewired and I can't do it.' He just laughed and said he would help. I promised him £10 a week and thankfully he did the lot. He rewired the entire theatre, with me as his lackey, we put a brand new state-of-the-art operations board too. It was magnificent and no one at the Pavilion was any the wiser. This real sparky then taught me how to work the board. On the night of The Pavilion relaunch, which was The Lex McLean Show, I said to the boss, 'Now I have to have a word with you Mr Docherty, because I'm doing a lot of work here and I'm still only getting £9 a week - I want a raise.' He told me to fuck off and I said 'Fine, I'll get a job at the King's Theatre now, because I'm the only person in Scotland who can work this new board.' He realised I had him by the short and curlies. So I got a raise on the spot.

2

JANETTE'S STORY

I was born May 16, 1947 and christened Janet Anderson, but because my granny was also a Janet they called me Janette. I lived in a council house in Mill Road, Queenzieburn beside Kilsyth on the outskirts of Glasgow and was an only child. My father was William Anderson from Kirkintilloch - himself an only child - but my mum Mary Kelly was one of 10.

My dad was a miner all his life and mum worked in an ammunition factory during the war.

Dad had actually been married before to a nurse who died in childbirth. The twins she was delivering sadly died too. I never found that out until I was 23. But although he had been married before, mum and dad were completely dedicated to each other. I had a lovely childhood and I went to Chapel Green Primary school. I was always small even when I went to school, I was the smallest there. I was a perfectly healthy baby and child. When I was born I was 8lbs. When I was about three the doctors said I wasn't growing very much. But back then they just said 'This is going to be a small one' there was nothing else they could do. When I went to school one of the nurses, who used to come around, you know a Nitty Nora, head explorer, decided to find out why I was so tiny. She sent me to Yorkhill Hospital when I was about six. I always remember that I was so small my wee legs wouldn't reach the floor even in primary one seats. I was perfectly in proportion, just tiny. They did loads of tests on me and eventually gave me a clean bill of health. Nowadays they would have given me growth hormones, but not in the 1950s. There's no condition or anything to label me with. I'm just small. All the boys at school used to call me 'the giant', which was funny. They'd say 'Oh here's the giant coming.' They weren't bullies and in fact I was never bullied at all.

I actually kept growing until I was 16, just at about a third of the rate of everyone else and stopped when I reached 4ft 5in.

When I went to Kilsyth Academy I was of course the smallest yet again. I loved the Academy and ended up taking a language and commercial course, doing shorthand, typing and bookkeeping. All the kids actually voted me class captain. I don't think it was a sympathy vote because I talked to everyone, always have, so I was friendly and knew them all. I didn't dislike many people, that continued right through my whole life. I also went to The Girl Guides and Sunday School and was a patrol leader, being in charge of the tents when we went camping. I had to sleep at the front of the tent and be in charge of these great big lassies - ME protecting THEM!

It looked like I had thousands of badges because my arms were so short.

But I actually got the performing bug when I was three. We had gone on a family holiday to the Isle of Man and there was music playing on the boat. My dad had one of those Brownie Cameras and took pictures of me dancing away in front of all the passengers. The funny thing was I was doing proper dance steps like a ballerina. I think everyone was amazed. When I was seven I started dancing lessons. I went to Georgie Grey school of dancing in Kirkintilloch. The classes were held in a little hut on the canal bank. It was two shillings for a tap lesson or two and six for a ballet lesson on a Saturday morning. I did both. All the other kids were taller than me of course, which meant they could never match me up with anyone for the routines so I always got the solo part. I did my first concert at Kirkintilloch Town Hall at seven where I sang the song Bimbo. The ironic thing about that is I had to wear a little boy's outfit, with a red cap, just like Jimmy Krankie would wear all those years later. It was the dancing teacher's idea, so she got me shorts, red cap and a bowtie - if only she knew what she'd started!

As soon as I put the outfit on I found it really easy to be a wee boy. No problems at all, which was amazing because I wasn't a tomboy at all. I was a cute, wee girlie.

At school the only real trouble I had was from a teacher Miss Hall when I did typing class. The typewriter was too high for me. She wouldn't give me a cushion to sit on, instead she would make me take a drawer out of her desk, turn it upside down and I had to sit on that. Of course the underside of the drawer was just rough wood so it would give me splinters in my legs. I said to her 'Miss Hall, this drawer is hurting my legs'. All she gave me was a yellow duster to put on top of it. I remember one day the drawer slipped off the seat and I went through the drawer, and I got into a row for breaking it - compassion was never one of her strong points.

I was an average student, but like everyone I got belted. It was always for talking, although it wasn't for cheeking the teachers back. You'd get belted for having a sweet, belted for yawning, they'd belt you for everything back then. But I finally left school at 16 with a commercial certificate and went for a few job interviews.

I had kept up my dancing during all that time and would entertain pensioners at old folk's homes in my spare time. I got turned down for a couple of jobs at the bank and council offices in Kirkintilloch. It could have been down to my height because they certainly weren't equal opportunities employers then. I then spotted an advert in the paper for a junior clerk for a company called Lion's Telephones in North Street in Glasgow. My mum came with me for the interview and I got that job. I started off filing, but I was so small I couldn't reach the top files, so they got me a little set of steps. When I was filing I was always singing away. There was a salesman in the office called Ron Robson who was married to Anne Fields - the sister-in-law of the Scottish entertainer Jimmy Logan.

Ron had been in a band called The Jones Boys in the 50s, so he'd had some experience of show business. He was the first person who ever said to me 'Have you ever thought of being in show business?' I didn't even know what he was talking about. He said 'My wife is in show business, her name is Anne Fields and I think you would also be great in show business too.' He then told me about a panto that was coming up called the World Of Widow Krankie with Jack Milroy at the Pavilion. There were roles for six children but they didn't want to use kids because of some new licensing laws. He then said that he was going to come out to Queenzieburn and have a little chat with my mum and dad. Well he rolled up outside our little council house in a great big blue Jaguar. My mother was beside herself and had the best china out for Ron and Anne coming to the house. Anne just looked like a star - fur coat, blonde hair, sheer elegance and my mum simply loved her. They both had a chat with my parents and asked if they could take me for an audition to the Gaiety Theatre in Ayr. I remember my first audition as if it was yesterday. I sang Baby Face, did a tap dance and I've been in the business ever since. I will also never forget my first wage from entertainment. I did 13 shows a week for 10 shillings a show - £6 10 shillings a week. At the office I was on £3 10 shillings a week, so with both jobs I had effectively tripled my wages. I was leaving Queenzieburn on the 7.45am bus, working at the office until 5.15pm, and then straight down to The Pavilion Theatre to do an 6.10pm and 8.40pm show, before rushing to get the last bus home - only to get up and do it all over again the next day.

I used to give my mum £3 dig's money and I saved everything else, although I did splash out on a few luxuries. The first was a white skin rabbit fur coat which I bought from Frasers - kids' size of course - and it cost me a whopping £30, a helluva lot of money back then.

I did three years with the famous Scots variety star Jack Milroy in The World Of Widow Krankie then Widow Krankies Hanky Panky and then Carry On Krankie. I got on well with Jack. Years later he came out on our boat, and asked me 'How much did I pay you when you started out?' I told him £6 10 shillings and he berated himself saying 'That was very mean'. But I loved the man to death and he was a great inspiration for my facial expressions.

Things used to happen to me in the show, like I would trip over my nightie on stage when all the Widow's kids were getting out of bed and he'd be like 'Keep that in' because it got a laugh. He encouraged me all the time and would include me in sketches too.

I kept up both jobs for two years, but was so exhausted I thought I couldn't do it anymore. I was then offered my first summer season which meant, combined with the panto, I could afford to go professional. So in 1963 I gave up the 9-5 office job for show business.

I never had many dreams or ambitions in my head at the time to be truthful. I am very much a live-for-the-day type of person. I still don't really plan for the future. If I'm doing a show then I've got to concentrate on that one thing only, I can't be thinking of lots of other things, like 'What does it all mean?' And 'Why are we on the earth?' That's all too complicated and stressful so I just think what will I do for the rest of the day when I wake up in the morning and little else.

During the summer season with Jack Milroy, one of the

musicians suggested to me and another Krankie Kid called Margaret Murray that we should get our own act together and try our luck at performing at the clubs in Manchester. It made sense because we had a break before panto started up again. He gave us some names of agents and we sent pictures of ourselves in little silver outfits wearing mini skirts and silver caps and braces. I always remember when I left home for Manchester when I was 18, my mum and dad got me to the Buchanan Street bus station and cried their eyes out. But they never once tried to stop me. Not once in my life did they attempt to put the blocks on what I was doing. But I never took advantage of them and they always just trusted me.

We found digs at Rosie Dylan's Guest House. Rosie was an old Irish woman, with teeth like a row of condemned buildings, but she was a great woman. Sometimes we'd get in from gigs at two in the morning and Rosie would leave us parcels of sandwiches with our name on it. If the musicians got in first though then your sandwiches - with your name on them or not - were gone.

Margaret and I would be doing the clubs, performing solo spots then teaming up together to do a bit of Scottish stuff, dancing and that kind of thing. We called ourselves the Krankie Kids. We originally went down to Manchester for a fortnight and stayed for 12 weeks.

The clubs were pretty seedy. One night the booker told us we'd be sharing the bill with 32 strippers, as he wanted to put us on as a novelty act. He asked if we'd mind if he changed our name on the billing to The Kinky Kids? So there's prim and proper Margaret and I sitting in this crowded dressing room with our matching blue cases surrounded by 32 naked strippers. This stripper said to me 'Can I borrow your lipstick love?' I said 'sure,' the next second she had lifted up her top and painted her nipples with my lipstick and went to hand me it back. I said 'It's alright, you can keep it.' All this time I would be writing home telling my mum everything was going fine. If only she knew!

The drag queens, strippers and comics were actually very protective of us and would walk us to the bus stop at midnight to make sure we got home alright. But Margaret and I loved it. The whole experience completely opened the eyes of this wee girl from Queenzieburn.

My family were never drinkers, but suddenly I was able to enjoy a wee tipple. We were never promiscuous or anything like that, even though I did end up with a boyfriend.

3

HOW CAN ANY GIRL RESIST A MERRY MAID TOFFEE?

Janette: Margaret and I had moved to another guest house in Manchester to be nearer the clubs when this Canadian soldier Jack turned up. He was quite tall and we were instantly attracted to each other, although we didn't have sex or anything like that. Just snogging. He was my first boyfriend. He was always talking about taking me over to Canada but we broke up when I returned to panto at The Pavilion in Goosey Goosey Glasgow with Johnny Beattie in 1965. That was the first time I met Ian, but lo and behold the Canadian turned up unannounced at my house at New Year. He was just a few weeks too late because I had started going out with Ian just before Christmas. So when he arrived I had no interest in him. But my mum felt sorry for him and I will never forget that the poor bugger had to sleep in my dad's caravan in the back garden in the freezing cold. I bet he wished he'd gone back to Canada instead of chasing me to Queenzieburn.

I met Ian while playing Johnny Beattie's daughter Jinty during the panto.

Ian was quite a smart and tidy wee boy. He always smelt of nice aftershave which was very unusual for the Pavilion stage crew at the time, believe me. He had pockets full of Merry Maid Caramels and used to throw these sweets at me on stage from the lightbox. I hated caramels but I would take them anyway - I'm sure there are names for people like him handing out sweeties to little girls. He then asked me out and we went to the pictures. Afterwards we went for a Chinese meal. Ian had paid for the cinema but I paid for the Chinese because I was on more money than him earning £9 a week, while Ian was on £6 10 shillings a week.

Ian's dad had a Ford Cortina which we used to borrow on a Sunday and go for a drive up to Fintry and have a meal at the Covenanters pub. But the funny thing was that Ian only got the car every alternate Sunday as he had to share it with his older brother Aiastair. Sometimes when we were winching we'd find a pair of knickers under the seat from Alistair's last date the weekend before. My favourite white rabbit fur coat would always come off over Ian's smart suits, so people always knew what we'd up to.

Ian: My randy brother had been dating almost the entire chorus line from that show. I think he'd worked his way through about seven of them and ended up marrying the last one, Jean Ambler.

But I was only throwing toffees at Janette because I fancied her rotten and also because I honestly thought she was the major talent of the show - however sickly that sounds, it's true. She was just different class and I'd never seen anything like her with all the visiting shows and acts that came in. Janette had charisma. She would have that Glasgow crowd in her hand and that's what I call true star quality.

At the time I was still seeing a girl named Irene McCann, who was a secretary at Scottish Opera. She was the total opposite from me and was very posh and sophisticated, or arty farty as I would say. I think we were both getting fed up with each other. She took me once to see some opera with all the luvvies, but I went to the bar and got absolutely pished and made a complete arse of myself. I think I started heckling the opera singers, that was after stumbling over half the audience while coming back to my seat late. That was my first and last experience of the opera.

After I asked Janette out, the band The Dallas Boys suggested we should all go skiing on the Sunday at Glenshee. We didn't have ski gear or anything like that and were all wearing our denims. I ended up skiing backwards into a burn and Janette had to help me dry off in the bus, holding my towel, I was bloody frozen. Janette at the time had taken a wee shine to my older brother Alistair, but after that day's skiing we hit it off - she obviously liked what she saw behind that towel even though it was freezing cold!

Janette: I fancied Ian's brother because on a Saturday matinee he used to come in and help change the scenery and I thought he was a bit of alright. He was even smoother than Ian. But we never went out as things developed with Ian after the ski trip. In fact on the way back on the bus Ian ended up singing something from West Side story and I realised that he had a great voice, that's when he told me he'd been in amateur dramatics. To be honest it wasn't some huge big love and first sight scenario. It was a gradual thing that we grew to really like each other.

Ian: But I knew I was going to have to cook for us both as soon as I realised Janette couldn't cook to save herself. She had taken me to her home in Queenzieburn and made me soup which was so thick the spoon could stand up in it. Ever since then the kitchen was always my domain.

Janette: Ian's got a real flair for cooking. He's amazing. He's the type who can taste any dish in a restaurant and know every ingredient that was used in it. He also knows how to improve them too. Anyway after panto I was asked to go to Edinburgh with Jack Milroy for the summer but because I'd been to

Manchester the year before I had a hunch that the show business scene was changing more into clubs and cabaret.

Ian: Janette had told me this so that's when we decided to get our own act together and would rehearse at Kilbowie Church Hall. We didn't really have a clue what we were going to do. I would open with a Sinatra song and I'd do stand-up before we started doing comedy together using props. Our first gig together was at The Strand in Glasgow which had cabaret acts with a compere. We went on as 'Jinty and Tough'. The best I can say is we were okay. Although it wasn't a particularly memorable occasion, Jack Short - who was Jimmy Logan's father - said to us afterwards 'I've got a big charity show on at the Metro' and he put us on. We did comedy lines to link songs and Janette danced.

Janette: We didn't have a structure to our show and didn't know where we were going, but somehow we stumbled our way through the performance at the Metro, and although we didn't exactly set the heather on fire, we hadn't embarrassed ourselves either. The only other gig we did in Glasgow was at Ian's mum and dad's silver wedding anniversary and that was it.

We would return to do the occasional club in Scotland in the mid-70s. But it was never one of our main stomping grounds. We'd only do a week at the most every year. We met the bingo owner Mr Goldstein in Jersey in 1975 who told us his bingo hall was falling away and he wanted to put us on doing cabaret. So we were booked to do the Mecca Bingo in Partick and in The Gorbals back in Glasgow.

Ian: For part of our act Janette used to dress up as a Womble. But to come in as a Womble, she had to go out a side door of the building, onto the street and come back in through the Bingo Hall.

Janette: As I was doing this in my full Womble costume, I ran past this drunk in the street, who had stopped in his tracks and was staring at me bleary eyed. I ran past him and never thought anything more of it. But our musical director Davie was having a pint and told us how a man ran into the pub and said to the barmaid 'Oh Jesus, geeze a large whisky.' She was like 'What's the matter?' And he said 'I just saw this bloody big rat running into the Bingo hall - honest to god it was about 4ft high'. Well they refused to serve him and threw him out on the street for having too much to drink.

Ian: In the Gorbals I was setting up my speakers on stage long before the show and there were four wee, hard Glaswegian women sitting at a table down below. With typical Glaswegian tact, one of them shouts 'Oi son, whit are ye daein?' I said 'I'm setting up my speakers - I'm the cabaret tonight'. And she shouts back 'Cabaret? Cabaret? Are you any fucking good?' Quick as a flash I replied 'If I was any fucking good I wouldn't be in here, would I?'. Well, she thought about it for a second and said 'Aye, you've got a point there son'.

Janette: But that was years later when we were more established. Back then we knew we had a lot to learn and in June of 1966 Ian and I headed to Manchester to work in the clubs.

Ian: We felt we had to move because Scotland at the time was a closed shop and the show business scene was run by just a handful of people. It was very hard to break through, especially doing what we were trying to do. So really we took a gamble and went south.

Janette: My mum and dad didn't have a problem with me going off with Ian as they really liked him. Ian actually got more hassle from his family than I did.

Ian: When I'd left for Manchester an aunt heard I'd gone with Janette and said to my father 'You shall go down there and drag him back up here.' She called me a disgrace to the family. Fortunately it didn't come to that. It's amazing because really that sort of attitude wasn't so long ago. Look how quickly the world and attitudes have changed. When we got to Manchester old Rosie Dylan wouldn't let us share a room together in her B&B unless we were married. So much for the swinging sixties.

Janette: The agent I had worked for previously got us gigs again, but some of them in horrendous places. I remember one the Del Sol, which was a real dive with black and white tiles everywhere, the place looked like a lavatory. It didn't open until one in the morning. We would do 14 shows a week for this agent and were on £6 a show, making £12 a night. Out of that we had to pay digs and the agent's fee, but we were still clearing £50 a week - the average wage in Britain was £12 a week at the time.

Ian: To be honest Manchester was too soon for us. The massive old English pubs were fine, but the clubs were a disaster as we were doing the hell holes. It was the era of the smoky jazz musicians playing in these big casinos. Then we came in singing Big Pearly Gates and that kind of shit - it didn't go down well at all.

Janette: An Italian manager at a club came up to us when we'd just started the act and said 'no, no, no, you're like a couple of Salvation Army children - I'm going to get rid of you.' and he sacked us on the opening night.

Ian: There were also some really heavy characters. There was one venue called Mr Smiths and the first night we were there, there were only five people in the crowd. I jokingly said to the manager 'How will you be able to afford us tonight.' He looked me in the eye and said 'Well on Saturday night you'll come back here and gamble and I shall get all my money back.' I naively said 'But we don't gamble.' And he replied 'You do now.'

Janette: Even though it could be rough we still liked the buzz of the clubs because we were just 19 turning 20. We were so happy just being together that we didn't mind the rough nights with these dodgy characters. We were of the opinion 'tomorrow's another day'. We also firmly believed that our act would get better. Put it this way, it couldn't get any worse.

Another act called The Two Gerrards from Hull were also staying in the same guest house as us. They were a real old style variety act. She used to come down in the morning in full make-up including blue eyeshadow and false eyelashes. She was also always stinking of Avon perfume that caught the back of your throat so much it was an effort to eat your breakfast. The other half of the act was Maori. But they suggested that we should come to Hull to start somewhere smaller to help develop our act. They were kind enough to put us up for three weeks before we got our own place. We rented a flat for £4 a week but again we couldn't tell the landlady that we weren't married so we pretended we were brother and sister.

There was no phone or anything and Ian would use the phonebox across the road as his own personal office. We were struggling badly for money at the time. Next door to us was a young teacher, who was quite new age and would smoke dope and that sort of thing. I remember one day we didn't have any money for coal and we were absolutely freezing. Ian had gone out and found this piece of fencing and chopped it up to light the fire and then we'd just go to bed to keep warm.

Ian: We also discovered that plenty of bonking was the best way to keep warm. But that didn't stop us from being hungry, so I actually used to go next door into this hippy teacher's garden and steal her cabbages during the day when she was at school. I also dug up her potatoes and carrots, believe me we were that desperate.

Janette: After we got a few more gigs we decided to invest in our first car so we could travel further for work. We bought this Vauxhall Victor for £60. It was maroon apart from a grey driver's door. We eventually got a week's work in the Spineymore Variety Club in Leeds. But our car broke down while driving from Hull to Leeds. We had to be there at 11am for the lunchtime show. The other problem was before the trip we didn't even have enough fuel for the trip so I had to pawn our radio just so we could fill the car up. When we broke down it was so cold I thought we were going to die from hypothermia.

Ian: I managed to find a garage and explained my problem to the mechanic and he repaired us for nothing and we were able to get to our gig, where we slept in the car park waiting for the venue to open.

Janette: On the second night when we were driving to the gig the car skidded on ice and we actually flipped three times. It seemed to last forever. In those days there weren't any seat belts and it was just bench seats so we ended up sitting on the roof of the car. One of the other acts on the bill, Bobby Jean and the Scot boys were behind us. Amazingly we were unscathed, just a little dizzy and Bobby Jean drove us on to the gig where we did our show.

Ian: We were dazed and confused but didn't want to lose the work, so didn't even think about cancelling.

Janette: Our old Vauxhall Victor was a write off so the next night Bobby Jean drove us to the gig and he ended up skidding and hit a wall. So I told Ian we're not opening our act with Open Up Those Pearly Gates ever again.

Ian: The working men's clubs were much better venues for us. They were busier for a start and people wanted to be entertained instead of being there to gamble.

Janette: We started using more visual props too and doing more chart songs like Rolf Harris's Tie Me Kangaroo down. I would use a giant wobble board which you couldn't see me behind until I popped my head up. That always got a laugh.

4

THE KRANKIES GO TO GERMANY

Janette: By the summer of 1967 the work had dried up and I called a contact called Bob Johnson who I'd met on my first stint in Manchester with Margaret. Bob was now working in Wiesbaden in Germany as the agent doing the entertainment for the armed forces, he gave us two months' work in the American bases. The two of us didn't have passports or had even been out of the country, but suddenly we were destined for Germany and after hastily getting our documents in order, we travelled by train.

But by this time we had all these props like the wobble board, a giant Mexican hat and huge bass drum. So we got off the train in Wiesbaden at six in the morning and promptly got arrested.

Ian: The police in this posh little place were all for running us out of town. We had stepped off our train with all our props and were immediately pounded on by two cops. They obviously thought we were a couple of vagabonds and they just started bawling at us, asking for our permits - or that's what it sounded like anyway - and I remember thinking to myself 'This is some welcoming committee.' Fortunately one of their superiors, who spoke English, turned up and after we explained, he apologised for the other two officers' behaviour and escorted us to our hotel.

Janette: The hotel was a huge place. It was the first time we'd ever seen duvets. Big puffy things, they were beautiful, and we couldn't stop rolling about in them.

Ian: But the big frauline manager used to give me terrible looks because she knew Janette and I were sharing a room and she thought Janette was just a little girl. So she had me pegged as some sort of pervert. Every morning she'd pet Janette on the head then scowl at me.

Janette: It was only when I had my 21st birthday at the hotel did she finally believe I wasn't a little girl and stopped giving me sweeties every morning.

Ian: Our contact in Germany was Charlie Koch who was a black Jewish agent from Miami. What we never realised was that we were entertaining American kids on their way to Vietnam. And when we moved to their bases in Turkey a few months later, we were performing to kids on their way back. They were just our age. It was tragic.

We worked with an American comic juggler called Terry Bergen. He said to us 'You guys are talking all wrong.' We were never bolshy bastards and would always listen to people. So Terry taught us the basics for speaking to these GIs, like saying 'the sidewalk' instead of the pavement and 'the trunk' instead of the boot of a car. He also told us 'Don't be frightened to talk back to the GIs' as they'll be shouting at us on stage. We'd never come across anything like that before where the audience actually shouted at you. He taught us some put downs for the hecklers like 'Why don't you stand next to the wall buddy, it's plastered too.' It worked. If you knocked them down they loved you.

Janette: We would do things like sing parodies of The Sound Of Music which was out at the time, 'I'm just 16 going on 17 - one day I'll reach two feet' the yanks loved all that stuff.

Ian: We were getting paid £80 a week, plus our travel - an absolute fortune. But we certainly earned our money when we went to Turkey. That was simply horrendous.

Janette: On the bill with us in the show was an English act called Terri Rogers who had had a sex change. Now Ian and I had never even heard the term 'sex change' before. But this fella had had all his bits cut off. On top of this she was now a ventriloquist - the best we've ever seen. She had one doll called Shorty Harris and another called Bobbie Kimber.

Ian: It turned out he had been a merchant seaman from Ipswich called Ivan Southgate who changed his name to Terri Rogers after the op. She had called one of dolls Bobbie Kimber after another English ventriloquist who had also been born a man but performed as a woman..

Janette: We went to Istanbul first and then travelled through the deserts in a Volkswagen van with Terri and a singing act called Michelle and Miles from Leeds. When we got to the Black Sea, Michelle and I went down to the beach. Terri came too but always wore a skirted bathing suit and Michelle and I would try to sneak a look to see if she had a willy. She had boobs and everything, but when we travelled overnight in the van the next morning Terri would have a five o' clock shadow.

Ian: We got to this God forsaken place in the middle of Turkey and arrived at the hotel reception, which was full of all these traditional Turks, in their traditional clothes, smoking pipes and Terri actually made the phone ring across the other side of the room by throwing her voice. She then did card tricks for the Turks and they were absolutely fascinated by her.

But after the gig when we were getting in the van, we were pelted with bricks. A huge gang of Turks had gathered and were trying to attack Terri. They thought she was a witch and wanted to kill her. Even the police were after her. Of course the bloody van wouldn't start and the crowd were swaying it back and forth trying to overturn us. We thought the worst. Suddenly it burst into life and we shot off through this sheep market, where the animals and the farmers literally had to jump out of our way as we escaped.

Janette: We would be eating in these awful cafes in the middle of nowhere. They'd be cooking things up in what looked like giant dustbins and we didn't have a clue what we were actually eating, but we were starving and had no choice. The food actually tasted beautiful, but it was guaranteed, no matter how tasty it was or where you ate, six hours later we'd all get the trots. It was hard going having the trots while travelling in a van over bumpy roads in the searing heat.

Ian: Having the runs was awful. I was so bad I was scared to fart. What's more, on the roads we were travelling they'd be rock falls, so quite often we had to get out and shift boulders just to continue - while all the time we were in severe danger of shitting ourselves.

Fortunately we ate really well in the American bases themselves. I had never seen a T-bone steak until I arrived there. I couldn't believe that one person could eat so much meat.

Janette: One time our van broke down and we had to get on the public buses with all our props and gear. All the locals would be sitting in silence staring at us. I swear this is true but the bus actually stopped at a field and two sheep got on. Just two sheep, no shepherd or anything. No one else on the bus batted an eyelid. We drove 10 miles down the road, stopped and the sheep got off without any encouragement at all. I'd never seen anything like it. Ian then leaned over to me and said 'You know when we go to get off this bus, there will probably be a pig driving it.'

Ian: We didn't even know where we were going or where we were. We ended up on the Iraq border one day, so we could have performed for a young Saddam Hussein for all we know.

Janette: But at the end of our tour we got engaged. Ian bought me a diamond ring from a jewellers in Istanbul and proposed on the boat crossing the Bosporus between Europe and Asia in June 1968.

Ian: It was probably the first and last romantic thing I've done in my life.

Janette: The only snag was about six months later when we were back home I was looking at my ring when I said to Ian 'My diamond's cracked.' He was like 'A diamond canny crack.' We took it to a local jeweller who told us it was just a piece of glass over solder. So Ian had been well and truly conned out of his £25!

We'd come back to Scotland to tell our parents we'd got engaged. My parents were delighted. They adored Ian. If I used to shout at Ian in the house, my mum would shout at me for ticking him off.

Ian: Mine weren't so happy, not because of Janette but because they were still worried about what I was doing in my life and because I didn't have a 'proper job'.

Janette: We were then offered another tour of Turkey the following year. After a fortnight you forget all the bad stuff because you're young and it was all one big adventure, so we agreed.

Ian: The train we took from Germany to Turkey was the original Orient Express. But the luxury chairs had been replaced by 12 inches of wooden slatted chairs. It got so hot we got sweat rashes.

One day we were stopped on the Bulgarian border. This was in the days of communism where the police woke you up by banging their guns on your arms. They ordered Terri to bring her suitcase down, which had her ventriloquist dummy inside. But she threw her voice and made it sound as if someone was trapped inside her case. Terri would open the case a little and 'the voice' would get louder. This policeman poked her case with his gun, then a big smile crept across his face. He loved her. He then asked where we were going and when we said we were going to entertain the Americans he said 'No you will entertain us'. He threatened to drag us all off the train so we could perform for the police. Fortunately we managed to talk our way out of it.

Janette: When we returned to England this time we got rid of the Hull flat and decided we'd live in the middle of the country so it was easier to travel. So we moved to Nottingham, then contacted an agent Jack Derman and started doing clubs in the Midlands.

Ian: Being in Germany and Turkey had given us a lot more confidence and we were definitely getting better. It was also great to be playing to a crowd once again when we weren't constantly having to fight the audience like we had to do with the Yanks.

Janette: We would do a lot of things called Shop Windows in the working men's clubs where we'd perform not only in front of the audience but for club bookers and agents too. We did one in Coventry one night in front of an agents' husband, Shamus Walsh. Shamus and his wife Joan have been our friends ever since. It broke our hearts when Shamus died in the Millennium year. He was the first man who genuinely saw something in us. Something more than just doing the working men's clubs.

Ian: He apparently went back to his wife and said 'I have just watched the funniest couple I think I've ever seen'. His wife came to see us the very next night. Joan was also a singer and with her contacts she introduced us to other people and a whole new circle of friends.

Janette: Joan gave us a lot of work for more money than we'd ever earned before. We were up to about £22 a night at this stage in 1969, which was really good going.

Ian: Coventry was also a great stamping ground for us

because it was so Scottish. We'd play pubs like The Tam O'Shanter which was jammed to the rafters with Scots desperate to see their own kind once again.

Janette: The beauty was they didn't want accordions and bagpipes - they just wanted a laugh.

Ian: But on top of that Joan and Shamus became our closest friends. We'd always stay with them if we were in the area. Shamus had also introduced us both to golf. For the first time since our self-imposed exile from Scotland, Shamus and Joan - along with golf - gave us a life outside of work.

Janette: Also when we told them we were getting married in October 1969 they were the first to buy us a wedding present.

Ian: But before we got married we were booked to go back and do the American bases in Turkey for a third time. This time we drove from Frankfurt to Turkey. But when we got to Bulgaria we had trouble with the communists yet again. They always seemed to be in the middle of some crisis or another and didn't want to let anyone through their country. They would put ridiculous demands on you like 'You're not coming through because your hair's too long.' They actually had a barber at the border crossing to cut these poor sod's hair. They said my hair was a disgrace. I wasn't exactly a hippy, we're only talking a bit over my ears. But I went through the rigmarole of having this barber trim my hair. It was just a way of humiliating you. They also would go through every part of your luggage with a fine tooth comb. They were really messing us about. The guy who was with us, Rick Caddy, was a good schemer. He found a young, smart looking police officer who looked more intelligent than the other officers. He then convinced him that if he ever came to our country we would not treat him the same way they were treating us now. This obviously struck a chord. This young officer snapped his fingers and we were instantly allowed to pack up and move on.

5

THE CHIMP WITH THE TROTS

Janette: On the third tour of Turkey was a Frenchman called Mr Louis who used a real Chimpanzee for his act. Ian was joking at the border if the police were going to cut the chimp's hair too.

Driving through Turkey it was boiling hot as usual and we had to stop at this lake one day just to cool down. We let the Chimp out the van and it immediately ran up a tree and wouldn't come back down. Even the ape didn't want to go back in the stinking, hot van. Another time when we stopped Ian and I went in the water for a swim to cool down. We were the only two people swimming in this lovely lake. But we soon found out why when this huge snake swam right past us. The lake was full of water asps. I told Ian 'Let's get out before we end up like Cleopatra'.

Ian: Even when we got out of the water onto the beach, the sand was alive with scorpions. When we arrived at the US nuclear military base in Dibaca, we told them where we'd been swimming. The soldiers looked horrified and said, 'No one swims in there man - it's deadly.'

Of course travelling through Turkey we all got the shits again. Even the Chimp had the trots.

Janette: As part of the Frenchman's act he used to dress this chimp up in a wee sailor's suit. One of the jokes was he would give the chimp a plastic potty and it would pretend to have a shit in it then empty it over someone's head in the audience.

Ian: Only this night the monkey didn't pretend because it really did have the runs like the rest of us. So it poured shit all over this big GIs' head. The GIs' mates were pissing themselves laughing. The whole place was in fits, but this humiliated GI gets up out of his chair covered in monkey shit and thumps another soldier who was laughing at him. Suddenly all hell broke loose and it ended up in one huge fist fight like in the Westerns - and all because this poor Chimp had the shits.

Another time after a gig I was having a break, sitting down in my kilt when this GI came up and said 'Are you a real-life Scotty?' I said 'Yip - the real thing.' Then asked 'How many of you are left?' I was like 'Look it's not like the Red Indians, we weren't wiped out.' He then asked 'Would you like to meet my friend, he was in show business too.' It turned out to be Johnny Paris from the band Johnny and the Hurricanes, I had all their records like Red River Rock. These guys were huge but their careers all stopped like Elvis the moment they went into the army.

Anyway, I asked these guys where the gents was because I was bursting for a pee and they pointed me towards these big doors. But when I went through the doors all these alarms started going off, it made a terrible din. Suddenly all these armed troops instantly appeared with guns at the ready. The sergeant took one look at me and told them that it was okay because I was just one of the acts from the UK. When I asked him where I'd wandered into, he said 'The place where we keep the heads - we're just 30 miles from the Russians here.' So I had stumbled upon nuclear warheads and The Krankies nearly caused an international incident during the height of the Cold War.

When we returned from Turkey to Germany, the dodgy agent Klopsy, who we found out later was actually Mafia, then asked us if we wanted a tour of Australia, Hong Kong, Kuala Lumpur and Saigon next and we said 'That sounds great.' But that night we were having a meal with a Cockney guy we knew and told him about the tour we'd been offered. He basically told us it was a load of rubbish, the place we would really be going to was Vietnam. He then handed us that day's newspaper and told me to have a read. It was all about the escalating troubles. We thought this agent wanted us to go to the Far East because we were so damned good, but the truth is he couldn't get anyone else so he thought he'd hire the naïve young Scots. Needless to say we didn't go.

Janette: In later years, after watching films like Apocalypse Now, we actually wished we had gone. I know that sounds strange, but it would have been an incredible experience. Imagine, 'The Krankies in Vietnam.'

Ian: When we told this agent that we didn't want to go he gave us some more work in Germany at another US base, but he asked us to take a parcel to one of the American Sergeants. To this day we don't know what was in that parcel and of course we were idiots for doing it - but we were young and daft. I reckon Klopsy had a ring of illegal gambling going at the bases, like Sergeant Bilko. It had been rife at that time until the Pentagon shut it all down. So I imagine we were carrying money for him in that parcel. Years later I was speaking to this black American cabaret act called The Clark Brothers and I told them about our experience with this parcel. They told me that Klopsy was famous for using cabaret acts to launder their money. It's a good one for the CV though isn't it: Money smuggler.

6
WE TIE THE KNOT

Janette: After Germany we returned home and got married, with the wedding at the Burnbrae Hotel in Bearsden. My mum and dad couldn't really afford it, but dad was determined to pay. We had about 110 guests for a beautiful sit-down meal and in 1969 it cost dad around £2,500, so he really pushed the boat out for us.

Ian: That wedding really did wipe her dad out, but he didn't give a damn because it was for his Janette. We spent our wedding night at Janette's parents' house and I'll never forget how naïve her mother was. I was sitting there watching the telly and Janette was packing up all the wedding presents to take back to our council house we'd just got in Peterlee in County Durham, and her old dear said to me 'When your father and I were married we couldn't wait to get up to the bedroom, but you two are sitting here watching the telly.' To give her dad credit, he leaned over and said 'Mary, they've been together for three and half years.' It came as a bit of a shock to her, she said 'Oh my God I never even thought of that.' She had come from much more innocent times.

Janette: The next day we drove to Peterlee and even did a gig that night. By that time we were working the North East every night as it was booming with clubs. Scotland was still in the dark ages at that point as the strict licensing laws wouldn't let anything open. The pubs still shut at 10pm sharp.

Ian: Of course because we'd been together for a few years and were married, it's only natural that the family started asking if we were going to have children. The honest truth is we never really thought about it. We never tried to have kids or tried not to have kids. We just got on with working.

Janette: We've never planned anything out in our life. Never once said 'Right it's time we started playing these types of clubs', or 'It's time to have children.' Ian and I simply aren't like that. The only thing we did plan at the time was trading in our Morris Oxford when we got married for a left hand drive Mercedes because Ian had always wanted a Merc.

Ian: The bloody thing turned out to have been a Portuguese taxi. It was a heap of shite. It blew up on the motorway shortly after I bought the bugger.

7

WE'RE OFFICIALLY THE KRANKIES

Janette: By this point we had a manager called Bob Dickledge, who managed the company Beverley Artists. He was booking 600 clubs at that time with huge acts like Roy Orbinson and Gene Pitney. Even in those days these big names worked both the social clubs and the night clubs.

Bob also told us that he couldn't sell Jinty and Tough, which was what we'd been going out on the circuit as, and told us from now on we were The Krankies.

The following year in 1970 Bob then sent us down to London for an audition for a summer season in Blackpool. We'd played in London before at Douglas House which was the headquarters for the American forces.

Ian: Unfortunately when we got there for the audition we immediately realised that the people we'd been sent to meet were gangsters - the white suit, black tie brigade. We actually got the summer season in Blackpool on the South Pier that summer. Top of the bill were Freddie And The Dreamers and we were bottom. The 'From Scotland' bit on the poster was in a bigger typeface than our name. We earned £50 a week which was a cut in money because we were earning a lot more at the clubs by that point.

Janette: We opened our act with the Frank and Nancy Sinatra song Something Stupid. The curtains would open and I was standing the same height as Ian on a platform with a long black and white dress, then half way through the song I used to step down and leave the dress standing.

Ian: The impact was instantaneous, it'd bring the house down.

Janette: We were in digs in Waterloo Road in Blackpool and instantly fell in love with the place as the buzz was incredible. We were always being invited to mayor's functions and civic receptions and the people really looked after us.

Ian: We were the youngsters so the other more established acts would take us under their wing. Tommy Steele and Mary Hopkins, Freddie Starr, Joseph Locke, Hilda Baker. These were names that we'd only heard of and they would come up to us and say 'Are you going to the party at the Lemon Tree tonight?' and we'd be like, 'We canny really afford it.' Everyone of them would tell us, 'Nonsense, you're coming.' They would pay for all our food and drinks, everything, because we were bottom of the bill and they'd all been there at some point in their lives.

Janette: Freddie Garretty, who had number hits at the time as Fredie and the Dreamers, used to take us to his mansion on a Sunday for dinner with his family. Ian and Freddie were about the same size so he would also give Ian all his old shirts and suits.

Ian: I had never seen a lifestyle like it. His garden had fountains and a swimming pool. I thought 'I want a bit of this.' Don't get me wrong though, they wouldn't be like that with everyone, because pros are pretty funny that way. They'll only take to you if they see talent in you. But once they see that they let you into their inner sanctum.

Janette: Freddie Starr was always offering to take me out to football matches. I used to be terrified of him because he drove his sports car so fast. He never tried anything on with me, I think he just liked me. But he has those really scary eyes and always called me 'Jan' and Ian was shortened to 'Ee'. Only a Scouser could find a way of shortening the name Ian.

By this time we had a bit of money and Ian thought it'd be fun to buy a dingy. So we bought a 12ft boat with a wee Mercury outboard engine. We didn't have anywhere to lock it up so we used to chain the engine to the end of our bed in the guest house. These musicians, who were staying with us, used to come in and say 'Bloody hell - what do you get up to at night?'

Years later we'd bump into the same guys and they'd still be going on about that outboard strapped to our bed.

Ian: That started our love affair with boats that would continue for 30 years, with our last a 36ft Grand Banks motor cruiser which we sold in 2002.

Janette: But back then we used to take our wee dingy up and down the river and potter about in it. It was a great way of spending your spare time in the afternoon. Life was definitely a lot of fun back then.

8
THE MAKING OF WEE JIMMY

Janette: We saw Jimmy Clitheroe in Scarborough the year before our first summer season in 1970. He was a little man who played a little boy. He used to have his own radio show called The Clitheroe Kid and had been a massive star, who had been discovered by George Formby and used to appear in his movies. It was Clitheroe we used to listen to when we were kids, but we never thought of doing an act in the same way.

Ian: An old comic Freddie Sales watched our act from the side of the stage and afterwards he asked us 'Can you take constructive criticism?' We said 'sure' because as I said we were always up for learning, especially from the old pros. He then told us 'You've got it all wrong.' This was a bit of a surprise because this particular night we thought we'd done really well. He then told me that I would 'never ever be a comic as long as I'm standing beside Janette, because with all due respect you just tell a gag, but I can get you a 100 people who tell gags - she's the funny one.'

Janette: Freddie then turned to me and said 'You're small, why don't you use your height more?' He then told me to find a character for my height. His suggestion was for me to dress up as a St Trinian school girl, but I thought that may be a bit tacky. But we knew what he meant, he just wanted us to change our whole act round.

Ian: Freddie wanted me to be the straight man. This was the complete opposite of everything we'd ever done. Up until then I was doing the funny lines and Janette was the clown.

Janette: We went back to Scotland before being booked for Barrow-in-Furness Labour club and only had two 20 minute segments to do on the night. One was visual comedy and one was doing our Scottish stuff, dancing and what have you. This club said they'd give us £22 but they needed three slots. So we racked our brains about what we were going to do. Back home at Ian's home in Clydebank we went up into the loft where we found his grandfather's boots, his little brother Colin's red school cap and blazer and his older brother Alistair's khaki shorts. It looked great as the boots were far too big for me and the blazer was too small and tight like Norman Wisdom. I still wear his grandfather Robert's boots to this day. So we went way back down to Barrow-in-Furness with a few school gags but still not much of a clue about what we were going to do.

To open the act Ian came out and said he'd sing a song. Just as he'd started I walked through the audience dressed as Jimmy and said 'Excuse me, what ye doin' up there mister - are you a group?' This woman said to me in the audience 'Eee sonny have you lost yer mam?' They really thought I was a little boy.

Ian: I knew from that moment we'd found a winner as the place erupted in fits of laughter. I remember afterwards saying to Janette 'I think this is better than anything we've ever done before.' That was just before our summer season in Blackpool in 1970. But we didn't take Jimmy to Blackpool with us because it was our first summer season and also because we thought the audience would be too sophisticated for that sort of act - stupid eh?

Janette: We were also a bit apprehensive because Jimmy Clitheroe was still on the go at the time and we didn't want to be seen as nicking his schoolboy act, even though it was very different as it was a woman dressing as a wee boy.

9
NEVER KROSS A KRANKIE

Ian: With all the dodgy folk we used to meet and work with I was surprised we didn't get into a really major incident sooner because we played some really tough venues. One of them was the Downhill in Sunderland - the toughest club in the North East of England, where they used to do strip shows on a Sunday morning. Some folk have no respect for the Sabbath!

Our comic friend Johnny Hammond told us of an incident he had been involved in when he arrived for his gig and loads of police were outside the Downhill. He was met at the door by a stripper who was hysterical. The police then explained to him 'Look we've got a problem, there's a man sitting inside with a gun on his table and we don't think he's mentally stable. What we'd like you to do is go out there and do your normal act and when you distract him we'll grab him.'

This was the hardest club to get a laugh in, in all of England. It was notorious for it. If you got past 12 minutes you were lucky. It was full of shipbuilders from Sunderland. They used to read their newspapers when you were on. Anyway Johnny goes out there and he's dying on his arse. As usual no one's laughing, except the lunatic with the gun on his table. Two policemen in boiler suits ask the gunman if they can sit beside him and before he could answer they grabbed him and marched him out.

Johnny was still on stage at this point and he shouts after them 'When you've finished with him you can come back for the rest of these bastards.'

We were playing a similar place called Comrades Social Club, or The Anti-Social Club as we renamed it. There was a strongman on the bill called Brutus. So we go on and we're only getting a smattering of applause, no laughter at all. Afterwards it's the turn of Brutus and he gets nothing either. He starts tearing a telephone directory and they're all shouting 'Piss off, we can all do that.' He comes off stage and the booker comes up to us and says 'Well bonny lad, you can clear off because you're shite and you're not getting any money.' The strongman said 'You booked me - you pay me.' The booker starts giving Brutus more verbal until the strongman picked him up with one hand and hung him on a coat hook on the back of the dressing room door. Brutus then got the booker's wallet out his jacket, took £12 and buggered off. We were pissing ourselves laughing but we eventually helped this irate booker down off the peg and he asked us to go on again since Brutus had left by this point. By the time we'd finished our third act the booker was absolutely steaming and he said to us 'Well if you think you're getting paid for that load of shite you can bugger off.' He owed us £18 and one thing led to another but basically I swung for him with a light stand.

The next minute this huge miner appears covered from head to toe in tattoos which were all spelt wrong, and he chucks us out.

Outside I was sitting in our new Zodiac car when I saw this pished booker staggering about the street - I ended up chasing him around the car park in my car.

But I still didn't get my money. They were awful clubs to play Sunderland - but they were also a great training ground.

Then on Christmas Eve we went to Millview in Sunderland and again the booker wouldn't give us the money because he needed it himself to buy presents. This guy was a big ex-policeman and he threatened to chuck me out on my arse. So Janette says 'lets go'. The next day I returned to try and get my money while Janette was sitting outside in the car - suddenly she saw me running up Sunderland beachfront being chased by this huge bloody ex-cop. We were really depressed because we hadn't got our money and were skint for Christmas.

Janette: A year later they actually booked us again. By this point we had built up a good following and were actually becoming a bit of a name on the scene. But there was no way I was going back to this club after the appalling way they'd treated us, but told them we'd do it. I said to Ian 'I'm going to make them sweat'. So I waited until half seven when the club was full and I phoned this big idiot and said 'It's Janette Krankie here' and he was all cheerful saying 'Oh hello bonny lass are you lost?' I said 'Oh no, we know exactly where your club is and frankly you can shove it up your arse.' This left him right in the thick of it. The crowd was getting restless by this point and we heard later he went onto stage and said 'The little Krankie is no coming - she told me to stuff my club up my arse.' It cost him a fortune having to pay everyone back. Revenge is definitely a dish best served cold.

10

IAN THUMPS PAUL DANIELS

Janette: Because we were gigging so much we got to meet a lot of fellow performers. In 1971 we did a season at the Derbyshire Miners Holiday Club and were on the bill with a stand-up called Joe Black who was an old theatre comic. We were supposed to do sketches with him, but it wasn't our humour at all. He was doing send-ups on Romeo and Juliet and we were, what I suppose you'd call, 'alternative' back then, doing songs from the charts and what have you.

On that same bill was a double act called The Gallan Sisters with a girl called Cheryl who eventually married Roger De Courcey. This was the first time we ever met Roger and Ian went for a round of golf with him. This was before Roger had Nookie Bear which brought him national TV fame. But before that he was a very good singer in London's West End.

Ian: I get on with most folk but I didn't like Roger at all when I first met him. He was a typical bolshy Londoner. After that round of golf I came back home in a filthy mood and said to Janette 'That man's not right for Cheryl. He was so rude to everyone on the golf course - including me - I felt like walking away.'

Janette: We later did a summer season with Roger and Duncan Norvelle at Bournemouth. Roger and Duncan didn't get on very well either as Roger was a real moan, moaning at everyone - including us. He said there were too many children in the audience because of us and it made it harder for him to control the crowd. He was basically having a tough time on stage, really struggling. One night, after a particularly poor performance, I was walking down a corridor backstage when I saw Roger getting hold of Nookie Bear and he booted the puppet as hard as he could against a wall. He then stood over the poor bear crumpled in a heap, and shouted 'You think one of us could getting a fucking laugh out there'.

About 10 minutes later, when he'd calmed down a bit, Roger chapped on my dressing room door and asked if he could borrow some eyeliner. I asked why and he showed me Nookie, with his nose all scraped - he needed my eyeliner to colour in his nose before going back on stage.

But Duncan Norvelle had just bought a brand new customised car, a Cosgrove Sierra, when they'd just come out. Duncan wanted to park it right outside his dressing room window so he could keep an eye on it. So he got a letter from the company manager warning him not to park it there as it was blocking the exit, but he still wouldn't move it. He then got a letter from the theatre manager again asking him to shift the car and eventually the promoter wrote too - but he STILL refused to move it.

It was causing a right stooshie so eventually Roger took Duncan aside and said 'Look Duncan, I used to be a bit like you, very headstrong and bombastic, but it got me nowhere', and Duncan replied 'Yes, but the difference between you and I Roger is that I've got talent'. Roger went ballistic and chased him out the theatre. They hated each other after that and no wonder.

It all came to a head when one night Duncan missed his

call to go on stage which meant Roger had to go on first, even though he was above Duncan on the bill, then Norvelle came on afterwards, which is simply not done. By rights - according to theatre etiquette - Duncan shouldn't have come on stage at all that night.

At the finale we all step forward with the whole cast, take our bow and as the curtain went down Roger punched Duncan right in the face, but they both had to quickly compose themselves as the curtain went straight back up again for the encore - it was like a comedy in itself.

Ian: Surprisingly over the years I got to like Roger a lot when I realised all his brashness was just a front.

Janette: When we did Derbyshire Miner's it was a 20 week long season. It was really hard work because the first eight weeks of the season we entertained the adults with learning disabilities.

I used to come through the audience as Jimmy, but the carers would tell me not to go near any of the audience who were wearing green badges because they were likely to lash out.

They would even give some of them injections to calm them down before we went on. One night, when I was walking down the aisle shouting 'Has anyone seen me mam?', this big female carer grabbed me by the arm and got her big syringe out ready to give me an injection. I was shouting 'I'm in the show, I'm in the show, don't give me a jab.'

In October of that year our agent at the time Billy Forest sent us to do a month of gigs in Jersey for the first time. Down there we worked for a man called Jimmy Muir who was from Partick in Glasgow and owned The Sunshine Hotel.

Paul Daniels had been there for the whole summer. I'd never come across him before but knew of him. He'd been supporting an Irish comic Val Mone but when we arrived Val had left by this point so we were now top of the bill for the first time - something I think Paul resented. Paul was a super act but personally he was such a bore. We were all living in the same hotel and he'd have a trick in every pocket. We'd be sitting in the bar having a conversation with some guest or one of the other acts and he'd butt in doing some bloody card trick.

After a month we were sick and tired of him and our patience had just about run out. One night he came over to our table and butted into our conversation as usual - that's when Ian told him to piss off.

Ian: It was as if he was always trying to prove himself and felt he needed to foist himself on people to show just how good he was. I was so annoyed after a month of being constantly pestered by him that something just snapped and I swung for him. I didn't hit him that badly, but he still went flying off the bar stool onto his arse. I had simply cracked. But amazingly a punch in the gob had no effect whatsoever on Paul.

I would actually play golf with him after that incident and he was still the same pesky wee man, doing tricks at every turn as if nothing had happened. But to give the man credit at the end of that run he even bought Janette and I going away presents. So he didn't bear grudges.

Janette: One of my good friends is a singer/dancer called Leah Bell who had been seriously injured in a car accident after she'd fallen asleep at the wheel. She was in hospital when Paul Daniels sent her flowers - this was years before he met Debbie McGee. The roses had a note asking her out on a date when she was fit. So when she went out for a meal with Paul for the first time, he said to her over dinner 'Will you marry me?' It was their first date. Leah said 'Paul I don't know you at all,' so he offered to take her to America for a three week holiday, no strings attached, just so she had an opportunity to get to know him and decide if she wanted to get married. Leah thought three weeks in America would also be a good recovery period for her after the accident and so off they went.

When she came back I asked her how she'd got on. She said

'Oh Janette, it was awful. Every morning I got up and we'd go down for breakfast and he'd have tricks out of every pocket for me and the other guests. I was that sick of him making my boiled egg disappear every morning I order a fucking fried one.'

She then told me that she got so pissed off with him she couldn't even last the whole holiday. Instead she just slipped a note under his door saying 'Paul you really are an amazing magician - you can even make your women disappear.'

Ian: I was actually in a society called The Water Rats with Paul. There's only 200 of us in the world and you have to wait until someone dies to get in.

The King Rats were people like Paul, Les Dawson, Danny La Rue and Bob Hope. You have to be asked to join. It's an organisation of entertainers who do work for charity. Buying kidney machines around the country for hospitals - but it's never publicised.

Janette: We were booked to go back to Jersey in the spring of 1972. In the Christmas of 1971 though we played at the British Forces bases around Europe with two dancers from The Sunshine Hotel. It was called Have a Krankie Kristmas. We toured all over with a Jewish agent called Mickey Hayes and his wife. Mickey had a terrible toupee and an old Mercedes that he drove us around in. Mickey said he suffered from asthma and not for love nor money could we get him to put the heating on in that bloody car. This was winter driving through Germany and we were sitting in the back of his car frozen solid.

Ian: We also had a singing and dancing act with us and Mickey would only stop at expensive motorway filling stations for food, so none of the acts could afford to eat. We were all starving and freezing.

It got so cold one day we decided to make a fire in the back of this old Mercedes. I got a fag packet and lit it and we were all warming our hands on it when Mickey says to is wife 'Mary, do you smell burning?' She was like 'Yes dear'. I said 'Don't worry yer arse Mickey, it's just a wee fire we've got going in the back here.'

Well he slammed on his brakes and threatened to chuck us all out on the Autobahn. Despite our protests the bugger still never turned on that bloody heater.

Janette: The digs we had on that tour in Germany were old nursing homes for some reason. We actually spent Christmas in one of those places. But we did what we could to make this draughty old place festive, cutting down a tree in the garden and decorating it the best we could.

We were in Hamlin one day on tour in the early part of 1972 and I went shopping as usual. Before I went off Ian said to me 'Now Janette, whatever you do, if you see a man with a flute don't follow him.'

We returned from Germany and immediately went off to Ireland as we had a load of gigs. We got there the day before Bloody Sunday in Northern Ireland and were staying in the Tudor Rooms Hotel in Dublin where the staff were so nice to us - but that all changed after the news started filtering through the next day. We were supposed to be flying out of Ireland that Sunday, but because of the trouble they closed Dublin airport and we had to go back to the hotel. As soon as we walked back in they were shouting at us 'It's all your fault - it's the Scottish Protestants who should have been shot' and that was just the staff. The very ones who'd been so nice to us the night before. The atmosphere was very tense and we were frightened.

Ian: One guest told us quite chillingly that we shouldn't step outside the hotel as we'd get lynched. At that very moment in Dublin they were trying to set fire to the British Embassy. Anything British, cars and what have you, were being trashed and burned, but we couldn't get out. So we had to get the boat from Dun Laoghaire to Holyhead. On our way there they were burning union jacks in the streets.

Janette: We had never been so happy to leave a place in all our lives. We were in a force nine gale during that ferry crossing and felt awful, with everyone throwing up, but we were just glad to get away.

11

THE KRANKIES AND THE US SUPERSTARS

Janette: In 1972 we decided not to do a summer season and concentrated on the big clubs where we'd be on the same bill as Roy Orbinson, Neil Sedaka, Gene Pitney, Frankie Lane - albeit we were doing the coffee slot in between their sets.

Ian: The Americans were the nicest top of the bill acts we'd ever met, except for The Everly Brothers, who were out their faces on drugs. It was so sad to see them struggle because they were totally blitzed. In a funny way it did us the world of good because we stole the show that night in front of a huge audience. They were all there to see The Everly Brothers but they started booing them when they couldn't even speak properly, never mind sing. I had bought everything they'd ever done and was a huge fan but they were horrendous. They were so bad they even fell out with each other. It was such a shame. But when we'd come back on we got a rapturous applause.

Janette: After that gig we started to climb up the bills. These cabaret clubs were huge. There was the Manchester Golden Garter, Jollees in Stoke-on-Trent, Talk Of The North, loads and loads of these fantastic clubs, where over 1,500 people would go for a meal in beautiful surroundings and dance to an eight piece band - it was real class and I loved them.

Ian: It was a great shame when these fabulous venues died away. I think ultimately the big American names killed them off. I remember Satchmo - Louis Armstrong - came over and charged £25,000 for one week's work from Berkeley Variety. Wakefield Variety up the road were like 'right we'll beat that' and paid Shirley Bassey £30,000. It's almost exactly the same situation many football clubs are in now, spending money they don't actually have.

Later on the club owners turned more to acts like us, who they could pay £2,000 for a week and still get 700 punters in.

Janette: We started off on £500 a week, doing seven days a week in these clubs until we introduced the girl dancers, then we became more like a big cabaret act. I loved those days.

Ian: They were the best of times. I'd love to be doing something like that again. The only place like it in Scotland was the Piccadilly in Glasgow's Sauchiehall Street, which is now Victoria's nightclub. But down south the place was full of them. We were rubbing shoulders with the greats of the business in these places like Tommy Cooper. It was a fantastic shop window for us.

Janette: We got drunk with Tommy in his dressing room one time. He'd never leave it when he wasn't on stage and he wouldn't let you go until you'd help him finish a bottle - or three.

Ian: I'll never forget the time at Baileys in Leicester where we worked with Tommy for a week and he said to us both on the first night 'What do you drink?' Janette said 'Whisky' and I said 'Dry Martini.' When we went to his dressing room after the show he had a bottle of each for us. It was a nightmare because he wanted you to stay until the last drop. The thing is he'd be in that dressing room until about four in the morning, long after the show, then he'd go home, have a meal, then go to bed until seven at night, get up, have his breakfast and go and do a gig. He completely turned his day upside down. He was nuts but great fun and a lovely big man.

Janette: Neil Sedaka was very nice to us too. We worked with him at the Wooky Hollow in Liverpool when he was going through a stage of not being quite as big as he was in his heyday. I remember he went berserk one day when he gave his band his musical arrangements and they spilled beer all over them, he hated unprofessionalism like that.

Neil was in Liverpool with his daughter who was 10 at the time and sang some of the act with him.

Ian: I remember his wee girl coming into our dressing room and she told you everything. I'd be like 'How are you?' and she'd say in her little American accent 'Oh mummy and daddy had a row today.' And nosy me would be like 'Wow, what were they rowing about?' But I was caught out when Neil shouted from outside our dressing room 'Honey come out of there and stop annoying people.' But the nicest of them all was Gene Pitney. He came up to us at a gig in Chester and said 'You're very funny. You two will become stars and I'll remind you both I told you that the next time I see you.'

Janette: I asked if I could buy an album from him and he gave it to us for nothing, then signed it 'Until the day you are stars. It was a pleasure to work with such an entertaining act.'

Ian: We met him about 10 years later while we were doing Blankety Blank with him and he came straight up to us and said 'What did I tell you guys?' So it was lovely that such a big name showed so much faith in us.

Janette: Those were great days performing at these magnificent clubs. You'd drive up to the venues thinking 'I wonder who we'll be on with tonight?' We'd arrive and a name like Frankie Laine would be up in lights and we'd both shout 'Yer beauty.'

12

BROTHEL KREEPING KRANKIES

Janette: In the early seventies we were in Leeds doing the Berkeley and staying in digs run by a posh Jewish lady. Engelbert Humperdinck used to stay at the same digs. She adored Engelbert and even named her dug after him. The way she ran her guest house was the lower down the bill you were the lower your bedroom was in the guest house. So when we started out we were literally sleeping in the basement, by the time we topped the bill at the Berkeley we were 'honoured' - so she told us - to be given Engelbert's room.

Ian: Yes, but you could have knocked us down with a feather when we found out that this posh guest house doubled as a brothel. It was a guest house by night when all the performers were in after the shows, and a brothel by day. This woman would never let you answer her phone or go out in the back garden where she had a huge shed. But there was a Welsh comic called Dave Swan staying there too and when we came back from a gig one night, he was like 'Let's have a look in that shed.' So we sneaked down and found the key and opened it up. Sure enough it was a fetish room with chains and belts and a harness hanging from the roof. Dave started roaring with laughter and woke up the entire neighbourhood. Every light in the house was going on and we had to rush back to our room before the landlady caught us. But she was obviously a high class hooker. You could just imagine her catering to the fetishes of chief constables and high court judges, which is the type of clientele she would have relished being an inverted snob.

Janette: When Ian and Dave discovered what was in that shed everything started to make sense. For example it was the only guest house I've ever been in anywhere in the world where they changed your sheets everyday. It suddenly dawned on us that our beds were obviously in use during the day when we were out at work.

But Wales also had some very strange digs for the entertainers. We stayed with Mrs Jones in Cardiff who told us 'I only have top of the bills staying here - never chorus line or musicians.' She then went on to give us the house rules, which were 'There are two toilets in this house, one upstairs and one downstairs - but don't use the upstairs one for solids.'

Ian: I asked her why she didn't like musicians and she said she'd once had a nasty experience with them. She then went on to explain 'These two boys turned up at the door from the new theatre and were lovely looking lads. I told them I only had one room left but they didn't mind sharing. So they went to their room and I thought I'd ask if they'd like a cup of tea and a slice of toast, but when I walked in I found them lying on the bed naked. Well I knew right away you see - drugs'. We were both killing ourselves laughing.

Janette: In 1973 we were working with an act called Nikki and Gerry. Nikki was a beautiful French singer and Gerry was a Belgian trombone player, who adored me for some reason. He'd always be saying 'Aw my little Janette, you're so lovely.' It turned out though poor Gerry had a major drink problem as we soon discovered when we did a whole season with them in Jersey - so he was probably looking at me while permanently pished.

Ian: I absolutely adored Jersey. It was such a different and relaxing place to live. I'd never seen things like people surfing before. It also had wonderful restaurants, clean seas and warm air. What a gorgeous place. The hotel managers would take us out to the best restaurants and they got us into fine wines. That's where we really got a taste for good living.

Janette: That was the first time I'd tried an oyster with champagne. Big Jimmy Muir - who owned The Sunshine Hotel - would take us out every Sunday. Because we did such a long season for him over many years this was the first time we had to start producing our own shows. You just couldn't do your same act as you had to find numbers for the dancers and that's when I started doing choreography for the first time, with all my dance school experience coming in very handy.

Ian: I'd be thinking up and writing sketches, so when a new film like Star Wars came out in 1977 we'd do that immediately.

Janette: I'd do R2-D2 or Bugsy Malone. It was wonderful training because every year we went back we had to have a whole new routine.

But in 1974 we didn't go back to Jersey for the summer as we did a season for Fred Pontins at Pontins Holiday Camp in Torquay where we shared a rented house with a comic called Alan Fox. One morning we had a phone call from the police asking to speak to Tommy Duffy, which was Alan's real name. His son had been knocked down and killed on his way to school and we had to go and tell Alan. His family came to stay during what was an awful time for them all. We spent the whole summer with this poor family in mourning. His wife was wailing all the time. They had a nine year old daughter and we'd take her out, just to get her away from it all.

Ian: That was a sad, sad time. I saw Alan have an audience in convulsions with tears running down his face. It was tragic. He was making people laugh while he was breaking his heart. I don't know how he could do that.

13

THE KRANKIES ARE ON TV

Ian: Later that same year in 1974 we made our first ever TV appearance on the Saturday night show called Wheeltappers and Shunters Social Club for Granada TV. We did the ventriloquist dummy act but because of tha TV appearance The Daily Record - which was at the time the biggest national newspaper in Scotland - did a two page spread on us. That was our first big interview. I was back in Glasgow and I popped into Lauders pub where I bumped into the famous Scots comic Chic Murray, who inspired people like Billy Connolly to go into stand-up. I got chatting with Chic and he said 'Are you busy?' I was like 'Not really,' so he said come with me. Chic had such a legendary dry sense of humour. We were walking through George Square when this guy was running past us with 20 parcels precariously balanced and Chic said 'Excuse me, do you have a light?' Well this guy put all these parcels down, got his matches out his pocket, when Chic then said 'You know, I think I should give up smoking' and just walked away. That was just Chic. He was like that all the time. He then spotted an American couple trying to take a picture of a monument so he went and stood right in front of their camera. After he'd finished fooling around we went into the Horseshoe Bar for a drink. I said 'What are you having Chic' knowing fine well getting a drink out of him was like blood from a stone. He just put his hand on my shoulder and said 'Don't be stupid, you don't buy a drink here today.' I asked 'Why?' And he replied 'How many times have you been on the middle pages in the Daily Record on the day you're about to be seen on television?' I was like 'Never'. 'Exactly,' he said tapping the side of his nose, 'Within three minutes every bastard in this bar will be queuing up to buy you a drink - and me as well.' And he was right. I ended up having a great afternoon with him on the piss.

By the time we returned to Jersey in 1975 we were packing out the Sunshine Hotel. I don't think we really knew what we were worth. We were just glad to be playing to a full house every night, not thinking that we were raking in a fortune for Jimmy, who was a pretty tight-fisted so and so. It'd only be at the end of the season when he'd buy us gold watches as a present that we began to think he was taking us for a bit of a ride.

Janette: We were still young and naïve, but he would always be keen for us to come back the next year and would say to me 'Make sure you keep taking the Smarties - my contraceptive pill - Janette as I don't want you getting pregnant.'

But the truth is we were also in love with Jersey and loved coming back. That summer of 1975 we also bought a bigger boat and after Sunday lunch we used to go out and have a bit of sex at sea - those were the days.

Ian: We were having a very passionate afternoon one day in the boat, when I looked up and suddenly I could see the French coast. I was shitting myself In case I didn't have enough fuel to get us back.

But we used to have it off everywhere in Jersey. There wasn't a place Janette and I hadn't 'christened' from the golf course to the High Street. It was amazing we never got caught.

That year we also met the comic and impressionist Dustin Gee, who had the same management company as us. Dustin was great but he was very off the wall. To me he was groundbreaking, doing things I'd never seen or heard before. He would be doing incredible impressions of David Bowie and Doctor Who. He would walk on stage to the Teddy Bear's picnic because he was a camp act. I'd never seen anyone try to carry off a camp act in a working man's club before and I was sure he'd be eaten alive - but he had the boldness to carry it off. He was one of the first of his kind.

Janette: We lived in Jimmy Muir's cottage and Dustin was in the high flats across from the hotel. We used to go to this beautiful beach everyday with Dustin and his boyfriend, who was a bit mentally unstable.

Ian: There was a café at the top of this beach, where you had to walk down the stairs to reach the waterside. Dustin would say to the café owners 'Would you like me to go down and sell ice lollies for you.' So he'd get the tray around his neck and walk around the beach - but with a difference because he was completely stark naked.

He had the tray covering his willy. It was only after people had bought their ice cream and he was walking away and they'd see his arse would realise he was naked.

Sometimes one of our musicians The Vicar - called that because his father was a vicar of course - would come out with us. He'd wear a vicar's collar and walk into the bingo hall. Bold as you like he'd go up onto stage and say into the microphone 'Yes my son, I think this is the place for you' - that was my queue to run on stage with a raincoat, flash all the old dears then we'd run outside, jump in the car and race away.

You could just imagine all these old dears afterwards going 'Was that the half time entertainment?' But I was always flashing people. In fact you could say that I was a serial flasher.

One night Dustin asked if Janette and I would come along

with him to judge a beauty pageant. I really didn't want to go because I hate these beauty contests as you take your life in your hands if you pick the wrong ones. Dustin always took his dog Sinbad with him. But he was always smoking joints so we'd get into his car full of smoke and even his dug was high.

Janette: Dustin then picks the ugliest girl as the winner. She really was a bit rough, but he made her feel great by saying she looked like Anne Margaret.

Ian: I swear the one he picked had a limp, squint eyes and missing teeth. But Dustin held her hand up and said 'My winner.' The place erupted in fury, they were throwing ashtrays at us, calling us all the names under the sun - we had to make a sharp exit.

But sadly the following season Dustin's boyfriend committed suicide by throwing himself off the high flats in Jersey.

Dustin himself died of a heart attack in 1986 after suffering from cardiomyopathy. He'd had a heart condition all his life but never told anyone. His mother told me at his funeral that he'd been born with an enlarged heart. It basically gave up because he had been using drugs, poppers or whatever they were. I felt he was a very frustrated guy. He got his big break when he did the Les Dennis and Dustin Gee show. That was an excellent show and he could mimic people like Robert Mitchum to a tee.

Janette: Dustin came and stayed with us once when we were living in Coventry. He was desperate to watch Princess Anne's wedding on our first colour television - he loved our new telly. We just sat there for hours with him and he was wonderful company. He's a great loss.

14

LOST AT SEA

Janette: We did a season on the Isle of Man during the blistering hot summer of 1976, where we met The Grumbleweeds. We took the boat with us too on the trailer and the show opened on my birthday on May 16 at the Palace Hotel which also had a huge casino. The Grumbleweeds were at The Lido which was also part of the casino. So we were in one show and they were in the other.

We were living in a place called Peel with our musical director Davie Squires. In the afternoon Davie would come out fishing with us. One day we were about two miles from the coast and I'm topless sunbathing up the front of the boat when at the back Davie shouts 'I've caught a big one here.' It was a beautiful 15lb cod and we went back and cooked it up - it was delicious.

So the next day we thought we'd go back to the same spot during this beautiful summer we were having and Davie caught another fish, but this time it was a massive conger eel. He reeled it in and I swear it was about five foot long with a head the thickness of a man's leg.

Ian shouts 'Davie cut the line, I can't afford to have this eel in the boat.' But as they've gone to get the clippers, this giant eel has whipped itself up into the boat. At the same time they've both jumped backwards and tipped me off the front of the boat into the water while topless. By now the boat's unstable with the weight of Davie and Ian at the back with the engine, so it's listing badly and starts filling with water.

Davie makes the quickest decision of his life when he says 'I'll swim for help' even though we were two miles from shore - and that was swimming through jellyfish the size of dustbin lids. So off Davie heads to shore. It was terrifying as everytime we tried to rest on the hull, it would sink below the surface. The bow would only come up about eight inches above the water for about 10 seconds which would give you a rest, then you had to swim away and wait for it to hopefully come back up again. So I told Ian to dive down and get a life jacket for himself.

Ian: But the conger eel was still inside the boat. It was stuck between the seats, with the hook and line in its mouth and it was trying to get loose. It's flapping about wildly all over the place - but my life jacket was right where he was. There was no way I could get it.

Janette: It turned out we were fishing over an old aeroplane wreck from World War II and the water was full of congers. Anyway Davie's swimming for the shore. It was dead calm and the water was lovely and meanwhile I went through every stage of emotion from laughing, crying, screaming and praying. I had no idea if someone was going to come and get us or not. But it turned out that someone had spotted us from the cliffs with binoculars and had phoned the lifeboat. Lo and behold we later found out that the lifeboat was delayed getting to us because there was a car parked across their launch - what idiot parks a car on a lifeboat launch?

When the lifeboat eventually came to us and they pulled us out of the water, I was of course still topless and the lifeboat man said to me 'Well, Wee Jimmy will never be the same to me again.'

All the lifeboat guys had been to the show and all the way back they were shouting to me 'So did you ever find Yer Mam Jimmy - or would you rather find your bikini top?' But the crew were great and wrapped me in tinfoil to keep me warm. They hooked the boat up to theirs and towed it, still submerged, back to Peel harbour - with the conger eel sill trapped inside the boat.

When we got into port the lifeboat man asked Ian 'Do you want this conger?' And Ian was like 'Nah, it won - let it go.' The lifeboat guy then said 'You do realise when it gets back to its friends it'll say 'Honestly she was this size'.

Ian: So a bloody conger eel sank our beautiful boat. We then discovered that Davie had been dragged off the beach by passers-by after swimming two miles to shore. He was sharing a flat with our drummer Ron who always used to cook Davie's dinner. Ron was always a dour bugger and when Davie stumbled into the cottage, Ron said 'Eee Davie you're late for your dinner.' And Davie said 'Ron you're lucky I'm here at all' and that was it. He didn't even tell him he'd swam two miles and nearly drowned. He just sat down and had his dinner.

Janette: That night Davie, who played the drums, bagpipes and accordion, couldn't stand up straight as he was so stiff from the mammoth swim. But that was the best performance of our lives. We were literally just so happy to be alive.

Ian: Sadly that wouldn't be our last trouble with boats. In 1984 we had just finished doing a series of summer shows with Roger De Courcey, The Tiller Girls, Al Dean and Duncan Norvelle when we decided to take my mother on holiday with us on our new boat, Cape Point.

One day Janette, our bass player Harvey Smith and my mother went out on Cape Point to Swanage and dropped anchor. It was a glorious afternoon and I went in for a swim, but when I climbed back onboard and went down to the front cabin, I noticed that there was something not right - maybe it was the way my shoes floated past me in knee-deep water which alerted my suspicions.

I ran up to the fly deck and told Janette and my mother that we had to head back to land as we'd sprung a 'little leak'. I then called the coast guard on my VHF radio, telling them I was taking on water. The lifeboat operator seemed to recognise my name, as by this time we'd been on the telly for a few years now, and launched boats from Poole, Bournemouth, Swanage and The Isle of Wight - I think they all wanted to see the Krankies drown.

By now I was feeling deeply embarrassed and decided I would try to

save the boat myself, but the water was coming in so fast by this time that all my pumps had packed up as the seawater had wiped out the electrics.

The coast guards were now alongside and were telling us to abandon ship. They were concerned that if the boat went down in this particularly deep stretch of water, we would be sucked down with it.

So I passed my mother over to the coast guard first and then the life boat man shouted 'Bring the child on next'. I was like 'That's no child - that's my wife!'

I was still determined to save the boat, as it had cost me a bloody fortune, and told them I would try and head for the nearest beach, Studland's Bay, so the coastguard said they would follow us in. I told Harvey to keep his eyes open for any rocks and Janette to keep reading the depth finder, as I tried to negotiate our way to safety.

But as we approached the beach, I could see my mother staring at the sunbathers. It took me a second to realise that the large crowd which had gathered to watch the rescue operation, were all completely nude - we had landed on a gay nudist beach.

I said to my mother 'Look at that - a beach full of tools and not a spanner in sight'.

We eventually pumped out the boat, bunged up the hole and were towed back to Poole - and left with a £7,000 insurance bill. As we had nowhere to stay we phoned Roger De Courcey and asked if we could kip with him until our boat was repaired. It wasn't long before he was up to his usual, moaning his face off about everything. I said to him one day 'Hey Roger, maybe you should get a boat 'cos we already call you Captain Grumpy'.

15

THE MAD FRENCHMAN

Ian: The Grumbleweeds became very good friends of ours. Graham Grumbleweed is a smashing guy and did excellent impressions of Tommy Cooper and Elvis and they also had a mad Scots roadie called Jimmy Gillespie.

Janette: We had an act on with our show which was this mad Frenchman - an absolute bampot - who did a plate spinning act with his gorgeous young 16-year-old daughter Chantelle. But this Grumbleweeds' roadie was knocking off with Chantelle.

Ian: As I always do with people I'm performing with, I asked this Frenchman if he wanted to come out fishing one day. We were on the boat again when a huge basking shark came past the boat - not uncommon for those waters. In fact I was used to seeing them all the time as the area is full of them, but this Frenchman suddenly produced a loaded handgun from his jacket and started shooting at the shark. I couldn't believe this nutter was walking around with a real gun. He was seriously off his trolley.

I was so dumbfounded I was lost for words. All I could

muster was 'There's no need to worry - basking sharks are plankton eaters' then quickly headed back to port.

Then one day he comes up to me and says in his heavy French accent 'I's thinks that someone is screwing my Chantelle - I think it is one of The Grumblepersons. I will fucking kill The Grumblepersons who is screwing my daughter. I shall cut his balls off'.

So I say to The Grumbleweeds 'Are any of you mucking around with the mad Frenchman's daughter, cos he's on to you'. They were all like 'Nope not me', when suddenly the voice of their Scots roadie Jimmy pipes up 'Well, I've sort of been with her - but she was desperate for it I couldnae keep her aff me'. I warned Jimmy that the Frenchman had a gun and would shoot him if he caught him.

But that night Jimmy couldn't help himself and went back to Chantelle's bedroom. Her dad obviously heard them at it and started banging on the door shouting 'Chantelle open up - I know you are in there screwing a Grumbleperson.'

Wee Jimmy had obviously paid no attention to my warning and immediately leapt out of the window before the Frenchman burst in. Unfortunately he fell through a perspex roof outside.

Without a word of a lie the next day the Frenchman marches into The Lido with his gun out. He starts shouting at The Grumbleweeds, 'I know that one of you bastards was screwing my Chantelle last night. Be a man and tell me who did it.' Jimmy is actually standing there with plasters over his head from falling through the perspex roof outside Chantelle's window, but her dad - being a bit unhinged - hasn't figured this out yet. But as no one owned up he left again still ranting about killing a 'Grumbleperson'.

It didn't stop there because the next night Chantelle's up on stage juggling and she's crap, I mean she's dropping everything - including her knickers as it turned out - all the time.

Our band starts putting signs up to the audience behind Chantelle giving odds on when she'll drop the next ball. The audience then started shouting 'I'll give you £4 at 5-1' all of them were having a real laugh - except Chantelle's dad who's still fuming.

I was in the casino on a break having a chat with Maurice Gibb from The Bee Gees - who would later tragically die on the operating table in January 2003.

Maurice was a local boy and cracking guy to have a beer with, but the next thing we see is my bass player running past me followed in hot pursuit by the Frenchman who's waving the gun around shouting 'I'm going to kill you.'

I said to the hotel manager, 'You've got to do something about this guy, he really is going to shoot someone with that gun.'

At that time a chap called Bob Sangster had been knocking off the Australia Prime Minister's wife, it was a huge scandal at the time. The island was covered with press looking for him. As it turned out when I'd been rescued by the lifeboat man I spotted this huge yacht in Peel Harbour and asked the lifeboat crew 'Who does that belong to?' They told me 'That's Sangster's - he's in hiding right now.'

I never paid it any more thought until bumping into the press in the car park while trying to save my bass player from the mad Frenchman. They asked me if I'd seen Sangster and I said sure 'I know exactly where he is - he's in Peel Harbour' and they ended up getting him. But I still saw Sangster gambling in the casino every night. It didn't stop him.

Janette: We saw everyone on the Isle of Man, from acts like Chuck Berry, Dr Hook, Status Quo and The Bee Gees. They were great performers, every single one of them.

Ian: We did an 18 week season that year which is a colossal amount of time - now ANY act would be lucky to get booked for two nights over there - it's sad.

Janette: At that time in our life we were just having a ball. Every single day was a laugh and we still had no drive to be stars or any of that rubbish. We were earning up to £800 a week in 1976, so why shouldn't we have been enjoying ourselves.

Ian: We also had control of the show and would discover people like Rose Marie, the Irish singer. We only hired Rose because our other singer coming over from Liverpool was caught with dope on the Isle Of Man, which was just plain stupid as they were still giving the birch for offences like that. So we were stuck for a singer, when I spotted Rose in a bar.

Janette: But we were always up to no good. There was an act called The Raffles, who were really prim and proper and quite aloof. So one night we replaced their microphones with vibrators..

Ian: That caused a huge barney - they were really upset over that one. They walked on stage and sidled up to the microphone stand not realising that the mics had all been replaced with vibrators - the whole audience was killing themselves laughing.

But we were also on the receiving end of the practical jokers too. Our bass player bought a dead conger eel for the last show and had it pulled on a piece of string across the stage to Janette - it completely freaked her out.

Janette: Last nights were always crazy. Ian used to sing this song Marching Through The Heather, but the bass player gave all the audience bits of heather when they came in and told them to throw it at Ian when he started singing that song - Ian was knee deep in heather.

16

JANETTE'S BAD DAY

Janette: After Isle Of Man we went back to cabaret and that was the first time we did Jollees in Stoke-on-Trent with Ken Dodd.

Ian: Dodd was a dead nice man, but his act went on forever and ever. He never knew when to stop.

Janette: It was a beautiful venue, with fresh fruit and flowers in our dressing room every night and closed circuit TV so you could see what was happening on stage. It was also a very special venue for Ian and I because that was where we were 'discovered' two years later (more about that later).

We still didn't have dancers with us, just a two piece band including Davie from the boat incident on the Isle Of Man and Ron the drummer.

The following year in 1977 we were sent to Guernsey for the summer, and later ended up living there for 14 years.

We worked for a guy Brian Paul and Julian Jorge who was a big fat man like an opera singer. There was also a black tap dancer called Joe Chisholm and four girl dancers. One of those girls married Paul Jones and later went on to star in the big TV hit series Widows. Another dancer was Amanda Smith, who was John Smith's daughter - the brewing giant. We didn't know this at the time as she was forever going shopping to Oxfam during the day and would make a big point of it.

Ian: I remember asking her if she'd ever been to Scotland and Amanda said 'Oh yes, daddy has an island in Scotland - he owns Jura.' That was the only time she let on. I asked what her dad thought of her in this business and she said 'He thinks it's fun and jolly like I do.' So the Smith's were apparently quite happy for their daughter to be working with the Krankies.

Janette: I became good friends with big Julian and one day the two of us went out shopping. But because Julian had this huge fat belly and because I'm so small, when I went to cross a road and step off the pavement I hadn't seen this car coming as it was totally eclipsed by the size of Julian's gut. So I was knocked down by a mini. I went right over the bonnet and landed on the road. Luckily it wasn't going very fast, but I was left in a state of shock.

Strangely all I could think of doing was getting the dinner in for that night, so after I dusted myself down and told everyone that I was okay, I headed off to the supermarket where I tried to get frozen peas out of the bottom of a big chest freezer - and promptly I fell in.

I must have been concussed as the supermarket manager ended up lifting me out of this freezer.

I trudged back home and Ian looked up from his paper and said 'You've been a while'. I burst into tears and said 'Oh Ian, first I was knocked down by a mini and then I was trapped in a freezer.'

He just looked up at me and said 'You're no safe to go out.'

Janette: By this time we had a little Sea Nymph which was 18ft long and had a little cabin so you could get shelter in it. But I never went out that year in Guernsey as I was still too frightened after the Isle Of Man incident so Ian used to take out all the men from the other acts for fishing and swimming. He got plenty of use out of it.

But it was a wonderful season. The shows didn't finish until 1am and afterwards we'd go back to someone's house and they'd be singing and dancing all night. It was a fantastic time. The funny thing is I always used to read in the tabloids about big showbiz parties with drugs going on, but I can honestly say that no one has ever offered us anything stronger than pot. There was no cocaine snorting or anything like that going on.

Ian: I've discussed this topic with guys like Russ Abbot and he's as baffled as we are about why people take it and even where they're getting it from, because in all our years we've never come across it. I'm sure it must have been more of a London thing.

However I admit that we were big drinkers. We had rented this gorgeous house which had peacocks and rabbits in the garden. On the number of occasions I forget to lock the door we'd come in steaming and the rabbits would be eating the bottom of our bed with a peacock in the corner - I'd be like 'Is that a peacock in our bedroom - or am I just pished Janette?'

But apart from those pesky rabbits, I loved the tranquillity of the place and the audiences were superb. The venue would be full of holidaymakers and locals in equal numbers. Guernsey also had a way of life that was more like the 1950s and we loved every moment of it.

Janette: The booker Brian Paul would three times a season hire a ferry and take the whole show to the Isle of Herm where the buffet and booze was laid on for us. We'd be swimming in this beautiful aquamarine sea. It was idyllic. At the end of that season we went back to the clubs and by this time we were top of the bill in the places we'd started out in like Talk Of The North and Jollees.

17

OUR BIG BREAK - THE ROYAL VARIETY SHOW

Janette: It was the manager of Talk Of The North, Joe Pullan, who suggested that we enter this competition for the Club Mirror which was a trade paper, where all the club owners put names forward about who they thought was the best club act. Well he put our name forward and we ended up winning the National Club Act of the Year, Comedy Section.

Princess Margaret was supposed to come to Jollees in Stoke-on-Trent to present the award to us, but she was ill, or too pished, so Lord Bernard Delfont, the big theatre impresario, came instead of Princess Margaret along with a critic from the Evening Standard.

When Lord Delfont was shaking our hands and presenting us with the award he said 'A man called Leslie Durridge from the Isle of Man told me about you two last year. I enjoyed you very much tonight and I hope to see you in London sometime soon.'

We honestly didn't think anymore about it. But three weeks later we had to do the show again in Wales for the TV, which meant Delfont had to come back again to re-enact giving us our award again. That night we were staying in this Country Club where Lord Delfont was staying too. We woke up in the morning with a card under our door which simply read 'Ring Lord D in the morning.'

Ian: He quite matter of factly told us we were going to be on The Royal Variety Show. But this was February and The Royal Variety wasn't until November and we were sworn to secrecy and weren't to tell anybody at all. That was the most painful 10 months of our lives. We were to be Delfont's big surprise and he didn't want anyone knowing. Freddie Starr had once been his surprise one year, Rod Hull and Emu had been his big surprise another year - and now that baton was passed to us.

Janette: We returned to Jersey to work for big Jimmy Muir once again but we couldn't even tell him that we're doing The Royal Variety. It was murder.

Ian: I didn't tell my mother either because I knew she would have told someone at The Clydebank News because she was always happy to tell anyone who would listen what her boy was up to next.

At that time the Channel Islands were attracting the big cabaret acts like The Black Abbots and Jimmy Muir was worried that we wouldn't be able to compete - but we did, and did really well that year.

Janette: We had a very young dancer Denise Gyngell, who was just 16 but would later go on to marry the millionaire record producer and Pop Idol judge Pete Waterman. But back then we became her guardians as she was just out of school. We were pretty respectable at that point as we'd stopped shagging on the boat and on the golf course.

Ian: This was the year Jimmy put us up in his own apartment, which was gorgeous. But this old Scottish woman who stayed above him, phoned up the authorities and said 'There are gypsies staying in the flat below, they keep coming in at 3am.'

We were in this really posh restaurant one Sunday for lunch when Janette spots this old dear who had complained about us. Well Janette walks straight over to her table and says 'Would you like to buy some pegs?'

Then in September we were rehearsing at Jimmy Muir's club for the act we were going to put on in the winter, when big Jimmy comes screeching up in his Jag and said 'Wee Janette, Wee Janette, David Jacobs has just been on the radio and has announced you're doing The Royal Variety Show.'

Janette: I was like ' I know Jimmy.' He fell silent for a moment then barked 'Why the hell didn't you bloody tell me? I would have put it on all the bill posters?' I said 'That's exactly why we couldn't tell you Jimmy.'

Ian: It was all over the papers and we did interviews on local TV - it was such a big deal back then. So after that, Janette goes up to his old bitch upstairs and says: 'If we're bloody good enough for the Queen Mother - we're bloody good enough to stay next to you.'

Janette: The last few months of that season we were on a high, drinking champagne and eating Oysters every night.

We spared no expense as we wanted to enjoy every second of our big moment. I had a dress made by an Italian in Jersey, and bought a white mink jacket, it was beautiful.

Our main home was still living semi-detached in Coventry, but London agents were now starting to get very interested in us.

Ian: We naively thought that they were interested in our career, but they weren't of course. They just wanted to make money. The only one who was genuinely interested in us was Stan Dallas. We'd met him 15 years before when he was with the Dallas Boys at the Pavilion in Glasgow.

Janette: Stan was phoning us up and saying 'You have just six minutes in The Royal Variety and we need to get new musical arrangements because there's also a 30 piece orchestra.

You must time your act to perfection and know exactly what you do.'

He told us to rehearse at any given opportunity, in the house if needs be. I remember one day during rehearsals I'm dressed as Wee Jimmy and Ian is in his kilt when there's a knock at the door. It was our insurance man, he must have thought 'What the hell are these two weirdos into?'

Ian: But disaster struck when I got to the London Palladium. Just when I was about to go out on stage in my kilt for the full dress rehearsals I was spotted by Andy Stewart - who was a veteran Scottish entertainer, famous for his hit song Donald Where's Yer Troosers. He went to the directors and said 'I will not have anybody on stage in a kilt before me.'

They came up to me and said 'You can't wear that outfit.' This was the day before the biggest show of our lives. I was literally in tears. I felt as helpless as a child. I walked out of the theatre in a daze and around the corner into Carnaby Street. I must have been looking so fed-up and miserable because out of the blue this man said to me 'What's the matter?' It was like a shoulder to cry. I told him the whole story - poured my heart out - and he dragged me into his shop.

It turned out he was a tailor and said, 'I will make you an outfit at my expense. It will be an honour to have my clothes on television in front of the Queen Mum.' This tailor made me a beautiful tartan jacket, it was absolutely exquisite. He saved the day for us because there was a gag about tartan in the act that we had so laboriously rehearsed that I would have had to ditch if I wasn't wearing tartan - which would in turn have thrown our timing out.

Andy Stewart had deliberately tried to kibosh me and I never really forgave him for that. I think he was annoyed that we weren't part of the Scottish scene. We hadn't come through the clubs in Scotland like he had and we were Lord Delfont's surprise act - and he didn't like that at all.

My dad died in 1975 on the operating table having a heart valve replaced. He never got to see us on The Royal Variety Show. He always worried about what the hell his son was going to do with his life. So we booked suites at The Savoy for Janette's mum and dad and my mum and brother. But what you have to remember is that Janette's parents were coming down from a mining village where they'd lived all their lives and had never been to London before, never mind The Savoy Hotel.

Janette: I phoned my parents at The Savoy from rehearsals to make sure they were alright and my mum said 'Aye everything's fine Janette, the man's let us into this room - but there's no bed.' I asked if there was another door in the room and she was like 'Aye, but I didn't want to try it in case it was someone else's room.' I could hear my dad try the other door in the background then shout 'Oh there's a bed in here - and a toilet.'

To be honest we couldn't really afford to go to such an extravagance, but we reckoned 'It's boom or bust'. If it's the best or worst night of our life we are still going to celebrate it in style.

Ian: We spent £2,000 in total, because we also bought two rows at the front of the theatre which cost £100 a ticket. That was for everyone who'd ever given us work - agents, bookers the lot, along with family and friends.

The night itself didn't get off to the best of starts. As I was waiting in the wings, I received my cue to walk on stage just as Danny La Rue was coming off. Danny handed me the microphone and said 'They're all bastards darling.' The first thing I saw was the Queen Mother in the royal box, who glanced at me, then checked her programme as if to say 'Who the hell is this?'

Janette: Then as I was walking through the audience at the start of the act dressed as Jimmy, I said to this big guy sitting smoking a cigar 'Excuse me have you seen me Mam' and he said 'Oh for God's sake speak English.'

Ian: I thought at this point the whole thing is going to go tits up. I quickly composed myself, took a deep breath and announced, 'Sorry ladies and gentleman there seems to be a noise out there in the theatre' and they could see me looking at Janette wandering about the aisles. The atmosphere had become almost hostile. Something outrageous had happened. Someone had stopped The Royal Variety Show and everyone was craning their necks to look at Wee Jimmy. I thought 'If this doesn't work, there's nowhere for me to hide.'

Janette: I was coming through the audience saying 'Where's me mam - is this the Bingo Hall?'

Ian: And I say 'No this is the Palladium'.

Janette: 'That's right - The Palladium Bingo Hall'.

Ian: She then looks at me...

Janette: And I say 'Are you a group?'

Ian: That was the first big laugh. I knew we had them then. I replied pointing at Jimmy 'Has anyone lost...this?'

Janette: We then did a gag that Lord Delfont had told us not to do after seeing us perform it in rehearsals. But I had told him 'Don't worry - Wee Jimmy will get away with it.'

Ian: The joke went 'Jimmy, what's five and five?'

Janette: I start using my fingers to count...

Ian: And I say 'Don't use your fingers.'

Janette: I put my hands in my pockets.

Ian: Again I say 'What's five and five?'

Janette: I start rummaging around in my short's pockets, smile and say 'Eleven!' The place collapsed in laughter. We had well and truly won them over. We were on a high and also did our ventriloquist act, where I sit on Ian's knee and he throws me about like a dummy.

We then finished with something else we'd also been told never to do, which was make any direct reference to the Queen Mother.

Ian: At the end of the act I say 'So have you found your mam?'

Janette: And I look up at the Royal Box and reply 'No, but I think I've seen me gran'.

We left the stage with the applause still ringing in our ears, got changed, then returned to the wings to watch the special act who was Gracie Fields that year. As she sang Sally the television cameras caught us both with tears running down my eyes. They were tears of both relief and joy.

Ian: During the royal line-up at the end of the show, The Queen Mother shook my hand and asked where I was from, 'Clydebank Mam', and she said 'Oh I used to go there to launch ships' and I said something daft like 'Yes, I used to wave my flag at you'. She gave me a little smile and moved onto Janette.

Janette: Obviously referring to the ventriloquist act she said to me 'You must be made of rubber my dear - that was wonderful.' All I could do was smile from ear to ear.

Ian: That night back at The Savoy we were partying until about five in the morning. We had a great night with everyone. The next day I'll never forget as the phone started ringing at 8.30am. It was the Daily Mail asking me 'How does it feel to wake up a star?'

Janette: Our heads were thumping so we didn't exactly feel like stars. Then lots of other calls started coming through - all the papers had wanted us to be outside the Palladium that morning for a photocall. They also wanted to know if it was Gracie Fields' voice which had made me start crying during her song Sally and I was like 'Nah, it was seeing my dad greetin' in the fourth row.'

Ian: But the morning after there was a state visit from the Prime Minister of India so we couldn't even get a taxi to the Palladium and had to get a tube instead. At Oxford Circus a taxi driver honked his horn at us and shouted 'Oi Jimmy, what's five and five - fucking brilliant', before giving us the thumbs-up and driving off. I was baffled. I started thinking, 'How did he know...' then I suddenly realised, if a London taxi driver knows who we are then the papers must be right - we really must have made it.

When we turned the corner we couldn't believe how many press were waiting for us outside The Palladium. We may have been on a high - but our heads were still banging from the night before.

Ian: The night after The Royal Variety Show we were doing a gig at St Helens Rugby Club and the manager said to us after the gig 'Right get your book out so I can get a date for you to come back.' I was like 'Well, you'll have to speak to our manager in London now for all that' and he started ranting 'Oh hit the big time now have we? One bloody appearance on TV and you're too good for us now?' We had been true to our word and played St Helens right after The Royal Variety Show, so he got a full house, but because we didn't know when and if we would be able to come back we were suddenly too big for our boots. There's just no pleasing some folk.

Janette: Soon afterwards we were signed up to do Darlington panto, which was one of the biggest and most prestigious pantos in the country. This was actually our first panto together and we did it with the Scouse comic Stan Boardman who was always going on about 'the Germeens' in his act.

Ian: It was Cinderella, put on by a London company called Gems who were a very, very camp company. We were playing The Broker's Men and Stan was Buttons.

Janette: Stan was just full of fun. He was sharing a dressing room with an old actor called Graham Squire, who used to take his boots off between acts but he was so old he couldn't get them back on again. Stan had to help him on with his boots after every single scene. This old actor also used to take up the entire dressing room with all his old make-up tubs leaving Stan about a foot of space to get ready in.

Stan got so fed up that one night he put a sign on the old

guy's back which said 'Ignore me - I'm nearly dead.' When the old fella walked out on stage everyone fell about laughing.

When he finished his act, old Graham said to us 'My goodness I went down a storm tonight - they love me.' So the next scene the old guy had to do, Stan put another sign on him which said 'I am now dead' the place erupted. Stan was always playing tricks.

Ian: Stan was on the TV show The Comedians at the time. But he was also famous for being thrown off the Des O'Connor talk show because he told the joke about 'Fokkers to the left of me and Fokkers to the right - and some of those Fokkers were flying Messerschmitts too.' It almost finished his television career - and to think that nowadays that would be considered tame.

Janette: He kept getting into trouble from the theatre bosses because he was always messing about. One night he collected manure from the ponies in the show and put it in Cinderella's glass slipper. When she put her foot in it all the shit splattered up her leg.

Ian: It was a great season for us because we had become so well known from The Royal Variety Show. Even before we opened the panto they actually extended the run by a further two weeks because of the demand. That's when you know you're on to a winner. We loved it.

Janette: The only thing that was slightly annoying was the producers were an acting company used to dealing with actors, so they made us do everything to rhythm. If we were walking down a flight of stairs it was 'left right, left right' and they would berate you in rehearsals for missing a step. They once told me 'On stage you would have walked right through a closed door there.' I said 'Don't worry on stage I would have seen the bloody door and opened it as I've never tried to walk through a closed door yet.'

Ian: But it was good fun, even though we were on less

money than we earned in Jersey the previous year, when we were earning £1,000 a week. We were top of the bill in that panto and were on £700.

Janette: After we finished the panto in the early part of 1979 we went out to Australia for the first time in the Spring. Because the big fat opera singer we had worked with in Guernsey was quite big in Australia - well he was big anywhere as the joke goes - and he booked us to work in Sydney for a month.

Ian: We had landed in Sydney when we were invited to do a television programme called The Mike Walsh Show. In the four weeks we were there they ended up getting us on every week. The Royal Variety Show was also shown the week we arrived. So we became a name Down Under without even really trying.

Janette: The money wasn't great but it was a fantastic experience, relaxing on Bondi Beach everyday - it was like Jersey with heat.

Ian: After The Royal Variety Show was broadcast, they'd be queuing for tickets at three in the afternoon - and we didn't go on until 9pm.

Janette: We started getting offers from other clubs, but some of them were pretty rough places like the Dark Toes Dogs Race Track.

Ian: The compere at Dark Toes Dogs said to us 'I will put you on at nine o'clock then on again at half 10 - I think.' I was like 'What do you mean by 'I think' and he explained it all depended on how long the dogs would take to run because the compere started the races too. It was literally a case of 'They're off' then he would run up from the track to introduce us.

18

THE KRANKIES DO DRUGS!

Janette: We returned from Australia to do the North Pier in Blackpool. But before that we did our first Cruise Ship performances on the Orianna. We did it for a fortnight, cruising around the Mediterranean. Tracy Farmer was with us on the cruise. She had worked as a juvenile dancer with us in Skegness in 1971, but now she was living in a squat in Stoke Newington in London. So she left this squat to come on a cruise with us. She loved living in the lap luxury for a change.

Ian: For our act I would say 'Now where have you been today Jimmy?'

Janette: 'The Pyramids at Alexandria'.

Ian: 'Did you like it? It's one of the seven wonders of the world'.

Janette: 'Aye once you've been you wonder why you bothered'. That got a big laugh as it was true. We had taken a trip to the pyramids in a horse and cart with this guy who had about three teeth in his head. He was also stinking - the horse smelled better than him. He wanted to take me to see Muhammad's tomb. When we got there he took me by the hand and tried to take me off to see Muhammad's toilet. I told him 'There's no way you're dragging Wee Jimmy into any toilet - now bugger off.

Ian: We had our first and last experience of drugs in Alexandria. The Scots engineer from the ship was telling us they sold good hash there, so I bought five quids worth from a guy in the street who literally had one eye and a big dagger. Before I could negotiate he'd taken my five pounds and thrown the stuff in my hand. I was shitting myself more about taking it back on board, but I had paid a fiver so I didn't want to throw it away. Anyway I plucked up the courage and sneaked it onboard the ship. I asked our musician Davie if he knew how to roll a joint but all we had was his pipe so we used that. In fact Davie used to walk around the deck amongst the passengers smoking this pot - he stunk the place out.

The Master-At-Arms even said to me 'You probably don't know this, but there's someone on board who's been smoking pot - the passengers have said they've smelt it on deck.' I had to prevent myself from bursting out laughing. But I composed myself and said 'Don't worry, we'll keep our eyes open.' And all the time it was my fiver's worth of stash.

Janette: I didn't try the pipe as by this point someone had found roll-ups. But Dougie, the ship's engineer, tried our stuff and told us we'd bought total garbage, real cheap stuff. He then warned us that the sniffer dogs would be searching the boat at Southampton and the best place to put our stash was in the morgue - as all big cruise liners have a morgue. He said the sniffer dogs won't go near the dead bodies. All the staff hid their stashes there.

Ian: Someone then joked that it'd be some story if we were caught. We were laughing at the headlines 'Royal Variety Show stars caught in dope smuggling scandal.' So I thought better of my dope in the morgue and flushed it down the bog instead.

Janette: But a bit of cheap hash, bought from a man with one eye and a dagger, was the strongest it ever got for The Krankies.

Ian: After the cruise we went to Blackpool and were on the bill with The Black Abbots - Russ Abbot and his group - along with Roy Walker and Les Dennis who was the opening act, who wasn't very good even back then.

Janette: Les was a very light entertainer and did impressions. But we got on really well with Russ.

Ian: Although when we did the hand overs he would claim we'd nicked his jokes. We did the famous 'five plus five' gag and afterwards he'd be like 'That was mine, I want to use that next time' for his scout boy act.

Janette: We'd say 'Well that's your privilege as you're top of the bill, but just remember where you nicked it from because we did it on The Royal Variety Show - so people know it's our gag.'

Ian: But Russ went ahead anyway and did our 'five plus five' gag on stage. He only did it once and realised he'd made a fool of himself as the crowd started murmuring 'That's The Krankies' gag'.

Janette: To be honest it was an old gag when we had used it. But it worked brilliantly with Wee Jimmy.

Ian: That aside, the show played to 142 consecutive sell-outs. Two shows a night - although that incredible success was in no way reflected in our pay packets. We just thought it was wonderful that Lord Delfont sent us a crate of champagne. That's what you think is great when you're young of course. Now I'd be more inclined to say 'Keep your champagne I'll just have 10 percent of the box office then I'll buy my own.'

It would take until 1982 when we got a deal like that, which is called 'a tickle' in the trade. Delfont would give us the last two rows of the theatre for ourselves if the venue sold out. So on top of your wages you got the money from about 100 seats, which could amount to fair whack.

But you're naïve at the start and pretty clueless about the people making money from you.

I spent my free time playing golf with Russ and the Black Abbots and Roy Walker who was an excellent player. It was a wonderful time. Blackpool let us join the Royal Lytham and St Annes for just £70 for the season.

Janette: It was always lovely to go to a town who really appreciated the acts. We were always going to functions and dinners. We rented a house across from Russ and when his wife wasn't there we used to cook for him. You became very close to the people you were working with because you were with them everyday for 23 weeks.

In 1980 we also did the Britannia Pier with Russ Great Yarmouth. At the end of the season the local mayor put on a dinner for us all to thank us for being there - but the old codger couldn't remember any of our names. So during his speech he said 'I'd just like to thank the tremendous acts for coming here this year including Russ Abbot and his Merry Men', instead of the Black Abbots, before adding 'And of course The WANKIES'.

There were 1,800 people at this function and they were in hysterics. The Mayor's wife was wearing this crimson frock and her face turned the same colour. We've been called a few things over the years but never The Wankies.

Ian: During that time we did a couple of TV appearances including appearing on Ronnie Corbett's show after he had personally invited us.

But I soon learned there are sharks wherever you look in this business. Before we went to Australia I had put an offer in for an old schoolhouse in Darlington. It was beautiful and we were looking forward to moving in when we returned. But while I was in Australia I got a phone call to say I'd lost the house - to my LAWYER. So after Blackpool we didn't have anywhere to stay.

Russ had introduced me to a financial man who sorted us out thank god because as an artist it was hard to get a mortgage. One bank manager told me that he didn't feel confident in lending me the money as he was in amateur dramatics he knew how unpredictable the business could be. But this new advisor got us a mortgage in minutes.

Janette: This guy also told us that we were about to start earning serious money - I don't know how he knew that - but he got us to open a pension fund which we'd never even thought about. He said it was all going to change when Thatcher came in. And he was right, she changed the entire pension structure when she was elected in 1979. So in a way it was Russ Abbot who made us financial sound.

Ian: Janette used to moan at me sometimes 'Why can we no buy this? And why can we no buy that? Why do we have to stick all this money into a pension fund?', and I said 'Because, one day we'll no be famous.'

We always knew that the bubble would burst at some point as it always does. This was even before we had our own television show. I just knew that one day we wouldn't be doing this anymore.

19

JIM DAVIDSON

Janette: At the end of 1979 we did the Babes In The Woods panto at Bristol's Hippodrome. That was where we met the great Jim Davidson.

Ian: He'd just won New Faces and was a total Jack the lad. In a funny way he was like a carbon copy of me from 10 years before, but whatever it was we instantly hit it off. I think he always wanted to be Scottish. His father was a Scot and he loved all things Scottish. He was fascinated about the stories I would tell of growing up in Glasgow. And I loved him because he was so daringly outrageous.

Janette: One night he came back on the train from London drinking brandy all the way. His opening scene was to enter as Simple Simon on a skateboard. But he was so drunk he couldn't stand, never mind get on the skateboard. That night we also had this sketch to do with a bench that would collapse. Jim had to fall down in front of the school teacher played by Melvin Hayes from It Ain't Half Hot Mum. Melvin then shouts 'Get up Simon' and Jim says 'No.' Melvin's next line was 'Why won't you get up Simon?' And loud as you like Jim replies, 'Because I'm fucking pissed'. The place erupted in laughter.

Ian: We were playing two robbers every night in front of 2,400 people, on stage with Ben Warriss who was one half of a double act Jimmy Jewel and Ben Warriss, who had been bigger than Morecambe and Wise in their day. Ben was playing The Sheriff Of Nottingham and was a great guy.

But it was Jim who was the real party animal, which suited us fine because back then we liked to party too. We were staying at the Holiday Inn but Jim couldn't stay there as he was banned from all Holiday Inns in Britain after he smashed the front window of one of them. They would let him in for a drink but he wasn't allowed to stay.

Janette: A typical night out with Jim would be to start in The Grapes Bar across the road from the theatre and when that shut we'd hit the night clubs. After they shut we'd then head to our hotel bar until at least four in the morning. We'd be absolutely smashed, but get up the next day for a matinee. It was brilliant.

Ian's brother Alistair came to see us once on his way to Saudi Arabia on a Monday night and we took him out to a club, not knowing that Monday night was gay night at this place. There were naked bodies everywhere in this place - beside the bar, jammed in toilet cubicles, you name it. Alistair had never seen anything like it and looked worried. But Jim said to Alistair 'Don't worry mate, just stick with me - you'll be alright.' A couple of minutes later we looked over at Alistair chatting away to Jim at the bar, unaware that Jim had his trousers and underpants down around his ankles.

Ian: Jim was totally starkers and all the while my brother didn't have a clue - we were pissing ourselves. But that was just Jim. He was a mad bugger. Another night he said to us 'Fancy going to Torquay?' It was two in the morning and I was like 'Who's going to drive us Jim' and he said 'My roadie Kevin'. Now Jim had the only roadie in history who didn't have a driver's licence. Jim had already lost his licence through drinking and driving, which also meant he couldn't insure his big Rolls Royce or buy road tax. In fact his road tax disc was just a Jeffreo Tull sticker. So we went through to a nightclub called Chaplains in Torquay which was a gangster's haunt. Unknown to me, Jim had been sleeping with the boss's daughter and was a bit apprehensive about going into this place because he had just dumped the girl.

So we pull up outside this place and there's nowhere to park so Jim just leaves the Roller in the middle of the street with the hazard lights on and says 'Let's go in for one drink and if it's crap we'll go somewhere else.'

I went up to the bar and ordered the drinks and the bar girl said 'Don't worry I'll bring your drinks over to your table.' She carried the round over, then picked up a pint from her tray and emptied it all over Jim's head - it was the girl he'd just dumped. Jim was completely soaked through. He jumped up and shouted a few verbals at her.

Suddenly these two huge Italian blokes appear out of nowhere. The older one said 'Are you mister Davidson from the theatre?'

Despite being soaked, Jim's still full of bravado and says 'Yeah - what of it?'

The big Italian was like 'You have insulted my daughter and that means you have insulted me - I'm going to kill you'.

I thought 'Oh no, here we go.' Jim needed to say something funny that would maybe defuse the situation. Instead he squares up to him and says 'I'm not scared of you.'

The Italian dad just smirked before replying 'Have you ever heard of Bristol Mafia? I AM the Bristol Mafia'.

Most people would have looked to make a quick exit at this point. But not our Jim, who gives it 'Yeah - well meet the Glasgow Mafia', and he points at me.

I literally looked over my shoulder to see who he was pointing at before it suddenly dawned he meant ME. Well we have never run so fast in all our lives. We belted up those stairs with these two huge Italian men in hot pursuit and sped away in Jim's Roller. Half way back to Bristol he turned to me and said 'We could have taken them!' I said 'Jim, I canny punch my way out of a wet paper bag' and he said 'Rubbish, everyone from Glasgow can fight'.

But any night out with Jim was always an unpredictable affair. He was superb fun - even if he did almost get me murdered by the Mafia.

Janette: Jim was one for holding big parties at the theatres, which were always wild affairs. We'd have pyjama parties, ghost parties, where we would tip over stage beds while there was usually a couple having sex in them at the time. All this took place in the venues and everyone, including all the stagehands, were invited.

Ian: This stage hand had got hold of an usherette and had disappeared up to the Royal Box for a quickie. Unbeknown to them, we got the entire cast and crew to sneak up to the circle above them, while Jim and I tiptoed into the light box. Just as this stage hand was going full pelt we turned the spotlight right on them, lighting up his bare, white bum going 10 to the dozen - the whole place applauded. I don't think that poor wee usherette ever showed her face again in the theatre. But if only the audience knew what went on after they left.

Another time I remember waking up at 3am in the bar, suddenly sobering up by this point with Jim in a crumpled heap beside me. He raised his head a little and asked 'Ian there's nothing to drink, nothing to drink at all?' But I reckoned I could get my arms through a little gap in the shutters of the bar, which I managed to do and seize a sherry bottle, which Jim and I promptly downed before passing out again. Even today when I see Jim he still says to me 'Hey Mr Krankie, pass me that sherry bottle'.

Janette: We were out drinking and partying nearly every night, something which you can only do when you're young. We were lucky though because at the Holiday Inn there was a pool and a sauna so you'd force yourself to get up in the morning and sweat out all the alcohol before the matinee in the afternoon.

Ian: It never stopped. We were like that at every panto for the next six years. It was a wild, wild time.

After the Bristol panto finished in early 1980, we went off to America for the first time. We had some money behind us at this point and had always wanted to go to Miami. That was some experience and we stayed in a suite in a top hotel, living like millionaires for a week. But it could be a bit dodgy because that was in the days when the Miami hotels were still all owned by the New York gangsters. I remember asking the receptionist if I could put some money in the hotel safe and the guy said 'I would hang onto it if I was you.'

I was like 'Why' because I didn't want to be walking around with all this money.

And he replied matter-of-factly 'Because the door of our safe was blown off last night.'

Janette: We returned from Miami in March to hit the cabaret circuit once again. At the time we were getting pretty big in that scene. In those days cabaret clubs never had any blue comics or anything like that. In fact the punters couldn't stand any bad language at all. The blue comics worked more in the Manchester strip clubs. But the cabaret circuit was the type of place you went for a special meal, anniversaries and birthdays and so on, so it was always a great crowd. We had done all those circuits before with Roy Orbinson and Gene Pitney - but now we were actually topping the bill.

Ian: It was incredible to be top of the bill in what we

thought were the best clubs in Britain like Talk Of Midlands, Heart Of The Midlands, Night Out Birmingham. To us it was a dream come true and it was all thanks to being on The Royal Variety Show. Ironically years later we would lose our top billing because we had gone into children's television. But more about that later.

20

THE CRACKERJACK! YEARS

Janette: We were in the middle of an 18 week season doing Great Yarmouth with Russ Abbot in 1980 when we got a call from our manager Stan Dallas to say that we had got Crackerjack!. Our agent Laurie Mansfield had negotiated our contract.

Ian: Everyone in the country knew Crackerjack!. It had been going on so long that I even remembered it as a child. Although, at that point we didn't realise it was in a slump. It had been going for 23 years when we took over.

Janette: The strange thing was we weren't really jumping for joy. I didn't think it would be right for us because Keith Harris had a primetime show on Saturday night, whereas Crackerjack! was five to five on a Friday night. Those feelings disappeared the day we arrived at the BBC studios and realised that they'd spent a lot of money on the show, as it wasn't actually made by Children's BBC but by their light entertainment department, which had a huge budget. So it was a high quality programme, with wonderful sets and even its own orchestra.

Ian: I wasn't very happy in our first week though, as all we were doing was taking over the exact same format from Peter

Glaze, Jan Hunt and Bernie Clifton. They were nice enough people but at the time Peter was in his 60s and Jan in her 40s - too old to be Children's presenters. I think the problem with them was they talked down to the kids and they thought that a custard pie in the face was all they needed to have a laugh.

Janette: Actually we were in our 30s at the time, which is old in comparison to today's children's presenters, but still a lot younger than our predecessors had been.

Ian: In our second week I realised something was drastically wrong with the show because the studio audience just wasn't right for us. I asked Robin Nash, who was this ex-RAF commander in charge of the audience, where he got the kids from and he told me they were all from the public schools. So they were all upper class plummy kids.

During the second show Stu Francis, who is from Bolton, asked one of these kids a question during the quiz Double Or Drop, and the child replied 'I can't understand a word you are saying, will you please speak English'.

Stu's face went bright red. I thought he was going to throttle the little brat.

That's when I complained to Nash that the children were horrendous. I said 'Why can't you get normal kids in from Shepherd's Bush and Wimbledon' and he was like 'Oh no, we tried that, but they make too much noise.'

But I put my foot down and the producer agreed and told Nash that it was time to open the door to other children, which was a huge relief. I also realised that we had no black kids or Asian kids, it was all just a bunch of little Timmys and Harriets.

The next week the entire feel of the show changed. It helped us take Crackerjack! from two and a half million viewers to nine and half million viewers in two years - one of the biggest climbs in television history.

Janette: It was some learning experience. It's not like today where film crews follow you around with a camera. Back then there were huge big static cameras, and you had to stand in a certain spot and remember which camera you were on. When you were walking across the floor you had to stop on a certain cross, but you'd be looking for the bloody cross all the time you were walking. So there were a lot of things we had to adapt to quickly.

Ian: On top of all that you had to remember your script, songs and what to do in the sketches as they didn't have autocue back then. The BBC was very strict that way. We would get pissed off with them. On a Monday they would have all the lighting and sound men come in and they would make you do the whole show. These dour bastards would never smile or laugh at anything. All they did was sit there stony faced, taking notes. They were basically the worst audience in the world and going through that every week was very demoralising.

One of the things we used to do in the show was the Good News and the Bad News. One day in rehearsals I got so fed up with these suits just taking notes I said 'The bad news is Jimmy Krankie has no willy', and Stu Francis said 'The good news is he's got a great big fucking pair of tits' - but we still didn't get a peep out one of these BBC bastards. A few moments later a lighting man piped up 'Is that sketch going in?'

Not one of them had a sense of humour. They were a nightmare. The BBC lot just weren't our type of people at all. I remember once getting into a lift full of people including the newsreader Moira Stewart. She was very nice because she was one of the few who actually said hello to us. So when I got in the lift I then said something like 'Going up - ladies' underwear' and Moira burst out laughing, but all these BBC types would be staring at their shoes. I thought to myself 'To hell with them', and I started pointing to one chap in a grey suit and saying out of the corner of my mouth to Moira 'That's the head of the BBC comedy unit? He's a laugh a minute'. Moira was desperately trying not to laugh.

But the Television Centre at Woodlane was a miserable place to work. In fact it was the worst place in the world to try and create comedy.

Ronnie Corbet had told me something which I didn't really believe until I saw it with my own eyes - the writer's and the musician's rooms at the BBC were in the basement of the building with no windows. The executive suites were on the eighth floor with plush offices and windows with panoramic views. One of our writer's Russell, was turning into a nervous wreck in that basement. He said 'They stick me in corner of a room and tell me to write, but I can't write without a window and staring at four fucking walls.' It was Dickensian.

Janette: Meanwhile we were still doing the cabaret shows. We'd record Crackerjack! on a Tuesday, be off Wednesday back on Thursday, Friday and Monday. We didn't have a flat in London and were still living in Coventry in the Midlands at that time. But we had to do the night clubs because they'd been booked in advance. So we'd get the 8am train on a Monday to London to be in for rehearsals at 10am till 5pm. Get the train back to Coventry, have our tea and go out to late night cabaret.

We actually needed the cabaret because the wages between us for Crackerjack! was £500 a week and out of that we had to pay for all our travelling expenses, hotels costs, food, the lot. After that we were left with nothing. In fact Crackerjack! cost us money.

Ian: But the one thing the commuting did was stop all the boozing and the parties. We were too knackered to do anything. We had to be so disciplined and go to bed whenever we could.

Janette: By the end of a 12 week run of TV shows I would find it hard to concentrate. I honestly thought 'There's no way I can learn another line'. But somehow we managed.

The first season of Crackerjack! was directed by John Hobbs who had directed Butterflies with Wendy Craig and Some

Mothers Do Have Them. He was a wonderful director but he had the personality of a bank manager.

For the next year of Crackerjack! they got us a guy called Paul Ciani who directed Top Of The Pops and The Kenny Everett shows and suddenly Crackerjack! took on a completely different look.

Ian: Paul allowed us much more leeway and would bring out our natural side. It was also Paul's idea that we do The Fan-Dabi-Dozi record - so it's his fault. As he'd directed Top Of The Pops he wanted more music involved in the shows and encouraged us to do a pop record.

At this point we were getting more and more bands on the show as the viewing figures started to rise, the record companies would put more of their acts forward.

Janette: We recorded the infamous Fan-Dabi-Dozi at a studio in Haddington, West Lothian with a producer Pete Kerr from Edinburgh and a Scots guitarist Duncan Findlay. But to this day we have never seen a penny from that record. We did an LP with them also called Fan-Dabi-Dozi but shortly after it was released the record company folded - whether we had something to do with that I don't know.

It may be hard to believe but Fan-Dabi-Dozi was actually our second album as we'd released one independently in 1976 called Two Sides Of The Krankies - you guessed it a mickey take of Pink Floyd's Dark Side Of The Moon.

In 1985 we'd end up doing our third - and thankfully - last album through Polydor. It was another collector's item called Krankies Go To Hollywood - ripping off, well you know who we were ripping off.

But we never saw money for any of the albums either. Or The Krankies annuals that the BBC put out every year and which seemed to be extremely popular stocking fillers. But that's show business. It has a great way of losing money for you everywhere you look. We were always being told 'Such and such had to be paid and the writer has so much of a cut' and on and on.

Janette: At the end of the first year of Crackerjack! we were appearing in the Robin Hood panto in Nottingham where we couldn't believe the reaction we were getting because of the telly. The kids used to follow us around the streets on our way to rehearsals. They'd be shouting Fan-Dabi-Dozi at me everywhere I went. It was unbelievable how quickly it had all changed for us. We had a whole new audience right across the entire country.

We'd do three shows a day and because we'd finished Crackerjack! we were back having a wild time again. Our home was only 40 minutes away in the car, but we'd usually be having such a great time we'd just stay in Nottingham.

Ian: We had a suite on permanent stand-by at the Albany Hotel. I'd just phone up and say 'We'll be staying tonight' and it was always there for us. We still weren't on a fortune but we did start appreciating the good life. We got a taste for it and wanted more.

Janette: We were working with Roy Hudd during that panto, who was going through a bad patch with his marriage at that time as he had met a girl dancer called Debbie during that show.

Ian: When the panto finished I asked Roy what he was doing next and he sighed and said 'I'm going on holiday with my wife up to Scotland. We'll have a great time - although you do know I'm a lying bastard.'

Janette: Apparently before going to Scotland he was driving through London and his wife asked him to stop so she could pick up a newspaper - and Roy saw on the bill poster outside the newsagents saying 'Roy Hudd's wife sues for divorce'.

Ian: He later told us his wife also threw a bucket of water over him at home and said 'That's what they do to dogs that can't stop mounting'.

Despite his marital problems he was great fun during panto. He actually used to strip completely naked at the side of the stage every night for costume changes and on the last night an old couple said to me 'Does Mr Hudd know that everyone in the wings can see him standing naked?' So for 14 weeks, twice a day everyone in the wings had seen him in the buff.

21

THE BIRTH OF THAT CATCHPHRASE

Ian: Just after we'd started Crackerjack!, The BBC were always telling us we needed a catchphrase. We actually didn't want a catchphrase as it seemed everyone had one at the time from Little and Large with their 'Brill', Stu Francis had a few including 'I could jump off a doll's house', and 'I could crush a grape', even Bruce Forsyth had his 'Give us a twirl' on the Generation Game. I was very reluctant because we had always thought If you canny get a laugh - get a catchphrase. But they were insistent. In fact every time we went into Television Centre, they would immediately ask if we'd come up with anything yet. It was starting to be a real hassle and a bit of a worry because we'd been racking our brains for weeks, coming up with truly terrible phrases.

Then one night we were travelling to a gig at Jollees in Stoke-on-Trent, with one of our dancers Karen Long in the car. We told her our problem and that despite months and months of trying, we had hopelessly failed to come up with a catchphrase. Karen thought for a second, then simply blurted out 'Fan-Dabi-Dozi'.

Janette and I both looked at each other in amazement then

asked 'How do you spell that?' Karen replied 'I don't bleedin' know, I've just made it up'. But we thought we'd give it a try for the first time the following Thursday when we recorded Crackerjack!. To be honest we used it in the show and never really thought it had made the slightest bit of impact until about two weeks later when the kid's letters started to arrive saying that 'Wee Jimmy was Fan-Dabi-Dozi'. We realised it was getting big when I picked up the Daily Record one day and the back page sports headline said something like 'Scotland Are Fan-Dabi-Dozi', to go with a match report on a rare win for our national football team.

Janette: Workmen regularly shout 'Fan-Dabi-Dozi' at me when I'm out in the street. I know some people may have found it really annoying, but I thought it was a great catchphrase. It just sums up 'fantastic' and 'brilliant' in the same word. Karen came up with it over 40 years ago now and there are still greeting cards with the phrase. So it definitely had staying power which is the mark of a great catchphrase as far as I'm concerned.

Ian: I don't think people necessarily think of us when they use it, it has just become part of their vocabulary. It's even been added to Collins Dictionary with the definition of "Informal - An expression of admiration or enthusiasm. Popularised by The Krankies, a Scottish comedy duo."

I only wish I'd patented it - but Karen's probably thinking the same.

22

DING DONGS

Janette: Showbiz is a notorious graveyard marriage and people are always curious about how we managed to stick together. Every interviewer on every chat show always tries to ask about our relationship. Jonathan Ross on his BBC TV panel show It's Only TV But We Like It in 2002 was typically straightforward when he asked 'So Janette, do you dress up as Wee Jimmy for Ian in the bedroom?' I've heard that one a million times and I just replied 'Oh no Jonathan - Ian prefers me to dress as Harry Potter'.

But now we feel it's right to clear up all the myths and rumours. The truth is we have always been together as a married couple, but that didn't stop us having fun with other people...especially at these wild parties and we sort of knew what each other was doing and with who, but we always ended up back in our own hotel suite or in the house together at the end of the night. They were never anything very serious. But it's fair to say that The Krankies weren't as pure as the driven snow.

Ian: It was never luvvy duvvy stuff with the others. We never had flings as such. It was just these incredible parties that would get out of hand. Janette might ask someone 'Where's

Ian?' and they would happily tell her I was in the room next door with a dancer.

Janette: No one took it seriously. It was all just good fun.

Ian: Good, filthy fun.

Janette: They really were crazy times.

Ian: Everyone was up to no good at these parties and we were no different.

Janette: To give you an idea of what we'd get up to, one time we went to this party and Ian put some cottage cheese from the buffet on the end of his willy and sandwiched it with two cream crackers, then proudly announced to everyone 'Look - I'm fucking crackers'.

Ian: After Nottingham we went out on tour with a show called The Palm Beach Review and I remember once running around in the buff wearing nothing but an egg shell on my willy. As I said, I was always stripping off.

Janette: One of the guys in this show was a magician called Eric Zee who looked like Liberace, with a big bouffant. He had a real leopard called Scorpio as part of his act. He also had an assistant called Angie and a leopard tamer called Rocky - so Ian had a little 'ding dong', as we called it, with Angie and I had a little ding dong with the leopard tamer Rocky.

I used to say to Ian 'You've been with that Angie again because you have glitter on your balls.'

Ian: And I'd say 'You smell of cat's piss so I know you've been with Rocky.' But there was never any real jealousy between us. If any jealousy started to creep in then we knew it had to stop. We both made sure of that.

I know it may sound strange to people, but show business is a very strange way of life. Working in the theatrical world, it wasn't unusual to wake up after a night out with all these people crashed out on the floor of our hotel room.

It wasn't just about sex though, that was just something that would happen, it was just about having a laugh with people.

I'll never forget when we got to Glasgow with this show at the Pavilion Theatre and Eric Zee said to me that his leopard needed a run. I asked the theatre manager Iain Gordon if it could have a run about inside the theatre and I promised him it wouldn't damage any of the seats, as its claws had all been cut and its teeth filed down, so it was fairly safe. Iain reluctantly agreed and told the wee woman who ran his box office, who would sit there knitting all day in between calls, that she wasn't to allow anyone into the theatre because there was a cat running around.

This is God's honest truth, about 10 minutes later a Rentokil man came in to change the mouse traps and said to this wee woman, 'Is it alright if I go in' and she said 'Aye, but mind there's a cat running aboot.' This Rentokil guy walked in, then came running out in a cold sweat shouting at this wee wifey 'CAT! CAT! That's a fucking tiger you've got running about in there.'

This wee woman simply said 'Aye, I telt ye.'

Janette: The beautiful singer Patti Boulaye was also part of that tour and every place we turned up, the newspapers always wanted a picture of Wee Jimmy, Patti and the leopard together. But I used to dread those photocalls as the leopard was always fairly well behaved - until it clapped eyes on Patti and wanted to rip her head off. So in all those pictures you'd see me and Patti looking very nervous and no wonder.

However, it was at the end of The Palm Beach Review that we decided that all the madness and our little 'ding dongs' with other people was going to have to stop. Because of the position we were now in, there was no way we could get away with it any longer. I mean if workmen were shouting Fan-Dabi-Dozi at me from building sites, it wasn't as if I'd be able to keep having 'ding dongs' with people like leopard tamers quiet forever.

Ian: It never crossed our mind at the time, but if The Sun or the News Of The World had got hold of that story back then we would have been finished. We'd have been booted out of television in disgrace.

Janette: I also think there was a little bit of jealousy starting to creep in too and that was no good. We decided to knock it on the head after that tour when we returned to our house in Coventry and the back door had jammed, swollen from all the rain. Ian put his elbow through the window pane trying to open the door and cut his arm really badly. We had to rush to the hospital because there was so much blood. On the way there I remember saying to Ian 'That's God punishing us for being so naughty'.

Ian: So while I was on my way to hospital we decided to call a halt to all our little bits of fun. It was just too easy to get carried away and all our 'ding dongs' were really just us being too self indulgent. It was living life in excess. But after cutting my arm it brought us back down to earth. It took that painful incident to happen in 1981 for us both to get a grip again. But I swear we have never split up or had a trial separation or any of that nonsense. That has never been an option.

Janette: The truth is we've always deeply loved each other.

Ian: Although we loved having a good time we also knew the good time had to have limits. It had to stop to keep what we have as a couple.

Janette: We were also worried that someone we'd met at these parties may want to make money out of us, especially when we became a name on TV. We were always expecting some blast from the past to appear in the newspapers saying 'I bedded Jimmy Krankie.'

There was one stage hand we met years and years later at the Bristol Hippodrome who'd been to all our pyjama parties and The Royal Box incident. We invited him up to the house in Guernsey for dinner and I told him that we'd become a bit paranoid about our past coming back to haunt us.

I'll never forget what this guy told us because it really took me aback. He said 'Look Janette, there's no way anyone would have said a thing. We all loved those crazy parties and loved you and Ian. You were great guys and all of us had far too much respect for you.' So I reckon because we always treated people the same, no matter if they were a stage hand or a big star, it probably meant it kept us out of the tabloids even during the height of our years living in excess.

Ian: We would have parties after making our no 'ding dong' pact together, but we would just be daft. I had stopped taking my clothes off by that point too and left the stripping to others. A guy called Al Dean joined the show, who was a grade one nutcase. He'd honestly go up to a woman at a bus stop and say 'Excuse me madam, but can I see your tits'. The woman would of course be outraged and Al would say in his defence 'I'm not a pervert I only want to see one of them.' Usually he was sent packing but he did cost me a tenner when he bet me he'd get a woman to show her tits on the Blackpool pier - lo and behold he managed it. I don't know what he said to this girl, but she flashed them in broad daylight. I was so surprised because he was the skinniest, ugliest looking bugger I've ever seen in my life.

Janette: He was so skinny that during his act he'd put a red balaclava over his head and say to the audience 'How's this for a match?' He'd then put a black one on and say 'How's this for a burnt match'.

Ian: I remember a show in Scarborough where we topped the bill. Stu Francis was our support and bottom of the bill was Joe Longthorne. Joe wouldn't really mix with any of us as he's from Gypsy stock. He'd pull up outside the theatre and five kids would get out the boot of his car - no kidding.

Janette: Joe followed me into my dressing room after a show one night and said to me 'Janette I really want to give you one'. I was taking my make-up off and said 'Oh, do you Joe? That's nice'. And he said 'Yes, but with you dressed as Jimmy.' I just called him a silly bugger and told him to clear off. To this day I don't know if he was being serious or not.

Ian: Joe was a really funny boy on stage, but very quiet and really a bit of a weird guy. Although I assure you Janette never did take him up on his indecent proposal.

Janette: But also on the bill with us during The Palm Beach review - where me and Ian had our 'ding dongs' - was an act called Nuts N' Bolts who were a comedy band with a big black guy, who were all pretty eccentric. They had a thing called a bomb tank - an explosion which would go off in the middle of their act. But once during a matinee it never went off.

Ian: It was still smouldering, so I put it out the window of the theatre and the bloody thing went off. BANG!. This is no word of a lie, it was so loud it actually started the yacht race at Brixham. So we unofficially started this prestigious annual event. It was eventually declared a false start, but that didn't stop the bomb squad descending on the theatre. The cops weren't too bloody happy with us.

For the gigs in Scarborough that year, we had hired a big bungalow where everyone would come to the party. Our dancer Karen Long brought her Ulster boyfriend over one night. He was really into smoking dope. Again I was a bit paranoid and said to Karen 'Look we're now children's TV stars - I simply can't have pot in the house. It would be the end of us'. We also had council officials and theatre managers coming and going to these parties, so she promised that her boyfriend would ditch the dope around us.

One time I made a huge pot of chilli con carne for 35 people. Stan Boardman turned up with Al Dean and as usual within an hour, Al had all his clothes off. By this time everyone ignored him as they were so used to this big bag of bones running around starkers.

But just when you thought Al's behaviour was getting a bit tired, he'd do something so outrageous it would take your breath. One time we were all at a function with the Lord Mayor of Yarmouth and Al peed in the mayor's pocket. He had been standing there chatting to the mayor for ages and simply whipped his willy out while they were in deep conversation and peed in his pocket. The mayor never knew. He must have wondered later how on earth he had ended up with a soaking wet jacket which smelled of wee.

But back to my party, I'm in the kitchen cooking the chilli and everyone else is in the front room watching some sci-fi video. Anyway I walked into this room to dish out the chilli and the smell of dope would have knocked you out. On top of that Al's running around in the buff like a mad man because he's now high as a kite and he doesn't need any encouragement to go bonkers. Even Karen's old mongrel was lying on its back with its legs lying limp by its side, from all the dope. This dog got up to go for a drink and it actually bounced off the walls in the corridor.

Meanwhile Stan Boardman has taken my chilli and stuffed it up Al's arse, so now he's running around naked with his arse on fire. The stoned dug thinks this is a great laugh and chases after Al, crashing into everything, trying to the lick the chilli out of his arse.

I looked at all this mayhem and I just closed the door behind me and went back into the kitchen. I was praying that no one from the council would turn up and fortunately they had some emergency meeting so the mayor couldn't make it.

But my younger brother Colin was there too. He was only 17 at the time and thought it'd be a laugh to take apart the kitchen sink.

Janette: The only problem was despite being the school Dux he couldn't put all the plumbing back together again.

Ian: Although he wasn't caring because one of our lovely young dancers took him outside to turn him into a man. We couldn't get that smile off his face for weeks.

When Janette and I got up the next morning there were bodies lying on every available inch of space. Karen and her boyfriend had slept in the loft on the fibreglass insulation, so they were itching like mad.

But when I left I got a huge bill from the owners for all the damage we'd caused. The letter also clearly stated that we would never be welcome there again. That was another wake-up call because I realised that to a newspaper that was a story - 'Krankies Wreck Bungalow'.

FOOTNOTE:

Ian: When our book was first released in 2004, this chapter created little more than a stir. It was mentioned on radio a few times and had featured in The Scottish edition of The Sun, but the English edition had shown no interest in running it at the time, even though The Scottish Sun had exclusive serialisation rights.

Fast forward to 2011 and we're doing a pre-recorded interview for Edi Stark on BBC Radio Scotland, when she asks if she can talk to us about this chapter in our book. Not a problem... or so we thought. We had nothing to hide and nothing to be ashamed of. But a freelance journalist was then given a preview of the interview and it ran on the front page of the Sunday Mail.

Janette: Everything we had said in the radio interview was then twisted. At one point I had said how Ian and I had "got a bit romantic" out at sea after a Sunday lunch and we nearly ended up in France, as we wrote earlier in this book.

Ian: But that wasn't swinging - that was with ourselves. We were only married two years at the time and were hot for each other like any other young married couple.

But the way the coverage came across it was as if we're still at it like two old swingers. We have never been to swingers' clubs or any of that nonsense. But we had been open and frank about having a short, wild spell, which we had called our dirty 30s.

By this point we were now in our 60s are were trending on Twitter - a platform we're not on and never use - and the "swingers" story was picked up by every red top in the land, including, ironically, by the English edition of The Sun, who had shown absolutely no interest when they had it exclusively presented to them on a plate in 2004.

We had also just started our run in the Robinson Crusoe panto with John Barrowman at Glasgow's Clyde Auditorium and even had some daft reporter from the Daily Record doorstepping us at the stage door. It was the last thing we needed for a family show.

Janette: I was so embarrassed going back into work, but I needn't have worried as the cast and crew just made one big joke of it all. They even had t-shirts and tea mugs made up with "I've been swinging with The Krankies."

Then during the scene where Ian and I are in bed with John Barrowman when I say 'We're like Morecambe and Wise as they slept in the same bed too,' John adlibbed 'Nah, there were just two of them — this is a threesome,' the crowd just loved it. It actually couldn't have gone better.

We had great support from fellow pros too. Bobby Davro texted to ask why he'd never been invited to any of our swingers parties, then I had other friends texting us saying they were GLAD they had never been invited.

But it had all been a thing of the past. Wee Jimmy may have once been a dirty wee boy - but he'd been on his best behaviour ever since.

Ian: Then in 2014 we were offered an acting role in the popular ITV sitcom Benidorm, where we were asked to play a couple of old swingers. We said yes. Well, if you can't beat them...

23

LES DAWSON

Janette: It was during Scarborough that we really got to know Les Dawson, who was working in Bridlington.

Ian: We'd met him before at the BBC when we were making Crackerjack! as he was big pals with Stu Francis. But in Scarborough Les offered to have us picked up in his stretch Mercedes limo and driven to his friend's boat in York. Les was a huge TV star at the time, although surprisingly he was by no means the biggest theatre draw. We were packing in the kids and families because we were new and classed as children's entertainers. But Les was playing a smaller theatre in Bridlington which wasn't the best of venues, and he told us ticket sales weren't brilliant either.

Janette: On this day out were our friends Eric, Maureen, Stu, Les, Ian and I. We got on at York and started the day with smoked trout and champagne. We had to go up all these locks in the canal, where the old women would be waving at Les. He was a gent because he would always invite the old dears on board, get them pissed as farts on champagne and deposit them slightly worse for wear further up the canal.

Ian: By the time they got off the boat these old dears would be steaming. Les did it all the time. He was just hysterical. He was always on and would do his whole range of characters all the time. He'd then get bored with that - although we weren't bored at all - and that's when he'd start inviting the pensioners on board. He would be talking to them exactly the way they talked, pretending to adjust his boobs, the whole bit. It's still one of the funniest days of my life.

Janette: I remember he was talking to these two OAPs and asked them how long they'd been coming to Bridlington and one said "40 years". Les was like "40 years? Why have you been coming to Bridlington for all that time?" And this woman said "Because it's flat." That was gold to Les and he'd use that in his act. He was great at observing people.

But we had a fantastic day out with him and by the end of the afternoon were pretty pissed ourselves. The only problem was we had a 10 past six and then a twenty to nine show to do. At about four o'clock we left York to be driven at breakneck speed in this limo back to the theatre in time.

Ian: We had to drop Les off first and he was so pissed he couldn't find his theatre. Our car had to go and do a U turn after Les had got out and he was still walking up and down Bridlington shouting 'They've moved the bloody theatre'. Les was actually late and there were all these people in their seats waiting for him.

Janette: I felt wrecked that night. We hadn't really eaten that much apart from the smoked trout, but we got there just in time. I then phoned Les after our warm up and asked how he was feeling. He said 'I think I've been on. But would you bloody believe it, this has been the first night the theatre has been packed and I can't even remember if I did well or not'.

Ian: We vowed we'd never get drunk before a show again. God knows how we got through it. Later the stage manager said we looked like we were on autopilot and he wasn't far wrong.

But it was worth it after spending such a fabulous day with Les. He really was a legend in every sense of the word.

Janette: The Floral Hall, where we were playing in Scarborough, had a very deep pit so the audience couldn't see the orchestra. Maurice Merry - who had worked with Gene Pitney - was the musical director and was great fun. He used to get kind of bored and would do things to try and put us off our stride. One night he even projected blue movies onto the wall below us which only the performers could see. He'd put signs up like 'Gobble, gobble, gobble', while another time he got this poster of Freddie Starr, cut out his mouth then put his willy through the hole to conduct the band.

Ian: I tell you some nights you had to be careful not to lose the plot. Imagine what it'd be like walking onto stage and someone is conducting the orchestra with his willy through the mouth of Freddie Starr - showbiz eh?

Janette: In August, after the summer season we had to record the new titles for our second series of Crackerjack!, with Chas and Dave who had written the new theme song - 'Get yourselves ready, come on hear you shout - it's Crackerjack!.'

Ian: By this point the BBC had now gone into a full ethnic drive, so it was compulsory to have kids from ethnic backgrounds in the title sequence which was a big change from a year ago when our audience was full of white middle class brats. However, since we were filming the scenes in Scarborough where we were still working, the BBC told me it was MY job to find kids for the titles. Well I didn't know any kids from ethnic backgrounds in Scarborough, but they said 'You want to film the titles up there - it's your job to find some.' Then I remembered, our local doctor was Indian and had a kid. So his boy came along for filming, but because he was outnumbered we shot the scene 10 times and moved him around the pack each time - to make it look like we had loads of ethnic kids. Well, it fooled the producers anyway, they didn't seem to notice it was the exact same child. But when we returned for the second series of Crackerjack!, a new producer wanted to change everything around.

Janette: They brought two young girl dancers in, Leigh Miles and Sally Ann Triplett.

Ian: They brought in a lot of fresh blood, who were full of enthusiasm and were lots of fun - the kids loved them immediately. They all seemed to work best with Janette, because instead of Wee Jimmy having to work alongside a big glamorous bird, he was now appearing with a couple of bubbly kids - it was perfect for the show. So the sketches suddenly became a lot better and more diverse. We'd do different things like restaurant sketches because up until then it had just been things like Robin Hood and all the pantomime stuff, but for telly it should be a lot different. The result was that the show instantly became funnier. That second series saw ratings soar up to nine and a half million viewers - at five to five on a Friday. If a prime-time show gets four million viewers nowadays it's deemed a huge success.

Janette: I can honestly say, hand on my heart, that although we became so called big names on TV, it didn't affect us at all. I swear I am the exact same person I've always been since I was a kid in Queenzieburn.

Ian: All that changed was our lifestyle, as we got a flat in London, although that was nothing to do with our pay increase from Crackerjack!. Despite ratings soaring to nearly 10 million, we only got a rise of £100 a week, which meant we were on £300 a week each - pocket change for today's EastEnders stars.

However, what it meant to us in real terms was we were now capable of earning £3,000 a week at the theatre. So the big money was starting to come in from those sources.

Janette: In 1982 we were at the Birmingham Hippodrome with Billy Dante, who was a renowned panto dame, while Ian and I were captain and mate doing a slosh scene with Billy, where he had to walk in and shout 'More paste' and we'd throw a bucket of paste over his head. Well one matinee he got his timing wrong and got the paste full in his face, swallowing half the bucket - suddenly his lunch made a dramatic and unexpected appearance on stage too.

Ian: It came up like a fountain, he was as sick as a dog - but the kids loved it. They thought it was part of the act.

Janette: That summer Ian said 'Do you fancy a Roller Janette?' I didn't because I hate those bloody things. Anyway he was determined to get one so we went up to this showroom to have a look at a second hand Rolls Royce. I was trying to put Ian off by saying 'I'd look stupid in a Roller - I'd need to sit on 20 cushions just to see out the windows'. We then took this horrible, golden green coloured Roller for a test drive, to Makro cash and carry, as it happens, so I could pick up some shopping. One of my friends Joan had come with us and she was larking about in the back, waving like the queen mother. Joan absolutely loved it. But I was furious. After we'd been to Makro we went for a Chinese before going on stage that night and I said to Ian 'I'm not happy with that stupid car - if you buy it I'm divorcing you'.

That was the one and only time I threatened Ian with divorce. So we never got a Roller and Ian bought a boat instead.

In that summer of 82, Russ Abbot had left The Black Abbots, so now it was our chance to close the bill. We were on at the North Pier and did two shows a night. The 6.10pm show would come out at 8.20pm, as the 8.40pm audience would start to come in. We used to look out of our dressing room window at all these people who looked like a colony of ants. It was a beautiful feeling to know they were coming to see us. That was a 1,800 seat venue and we did 142 consecutive sell-outs in one season alone. We did great business there.

Apparently Paul O'Grady, who played Lily Savage, did the North Pier years later and he wrote about Blackpool in a newspaper article saying that his favourite memory from the North Pier was the time he met me! I was chuffed to bits when I read that, but to be honest it was all news to me. He then explained that I was walking up the pier to the show and he got talking to me and apparently we went to a café for a cup of tea. Although I don't remember Paul, it's the kind of thing I do all the time. If someone was chatting away to me and I had the time I'd happily go off for a cuppa with them. So I was amazed to read that he loved Blackpool so much because of our chat.

Paul wasn't the only one to have fond memories of the North Pier though. One year this woman came up to me and said 'Do you remember me?' And I was like 'No', because I'm always honest that way and won't try to bluff it. She said 'From the North Pier from 10 years ago'. I'm racking my brains saying 'Oh did you work in the show?'

She said, 'No'.

'Did you own a shop on the Pier?'

Again 'No'.

She wasn't helping me out at all so I asked straight out 'Well, how would I know you then?'

And she said, 'You walked down the Pier with me after a show'. And that was it. As I said hundreds of people would speak to us after shows. We'd be signing autographs for 40 minutes after every performance. But if someone like that lady or Paul O'Grady remember talking to us then I'm just glad we made such a lasting impression on them.

Before our panto season, we went out to Northern Germany touring the army bases performing for the families of the British forces. We were staying in a lodge near Hanover with two girl dancers including Zoe Nicholas, Bradley Walsh and a contortionist called Fluke. But every base we went to the army always cooked a special curry dish for us before the show. After a week we were sick to death of all these curries so we started stealing Fluke's food because she was a vegan and had everything specially prepared for her - so we all became vegans too.

The mountain lodge where we were staying was lovely. Well, lovely until we burnt it down.

One of our dancers was dating our trombone player at the time and one night when they got back for a snuggle in the lounge it was freezing cold so the musician decided to light the fire - unfortunately the fireplace was just for effect, it was a fake chimney. The smoke filled up the entire lodge, setting off all the alarms, it was so thick you could barely see. Ian woke up coughing and the stench was unbelievable.

Ian: The next morning the German owner arrived and he was furious. It didn't help when Bradley Walsh came down for breakfast singing Smoke Gets In Your Eyes. The German blew up, calling us all hooligans then he threw us out - in all the confusion I left behind four suits. So in one part of Germany The Krankies have been banned.

But we had the last laugh as the owner had set up an honesty box for the booze saying 'I'll trust you with the bar' - which is the worst thing you can say to a bunch of musicians - it's like a red rag to a bull and they drank him dry.

So we were the perfect house guests, drank all his booze and burnt his house down.

Janette: But the shows themselves were great to do as all the kids and the families loved to be entertained by acts from home. Then we were always made guests of honour at the regimental dinners afterwards - the army certainly knows how to look after you.

Ian: The troops liked us because we were a family act, but Bradley Walsh was just starting out at the time and didn't quite know what sort of act to do. It was a bit weird as he used to come on with an ironing board and set it up on stage for his act, but not do anything with it. He'd then ask the audience what they wanted to talk about. To be honest his act didn't work on the army bases. That was the only time we worked with him so I presume he must have gotten a lot better since he seems to be on absolutely every TV show today.

Janette: We did the panto in 1982 in Oxford with Danny O'Dea, who played the old blind man Eli from Last Of The Summer Wine. He must have been in his late 70s at the time.

I remember every night we used to drag him out. We'd be like 'Come on Danny, we're going to the pub then the night club' and he'd say 'No, I'm going home'. But he would end up coming out with us. It was a really cold winter that year with thick snow and we were staying in the Randolph Hotel and Danny was staying in some B&B up the road.

Ian: We took him to a reggae club and he loved dancing away with all the black girls. He was a great character. He told us once about these digs he had in Middlesbrough. The landlady said to him 'I hear you're playing tonight Mr O'Dea, well I'll know if you're any good in the morning because my next door neighbour goes to all the shows'. The next morning, she brought him some tea and toast in bed and said, 'My neighbour said you were very funny last night,' then without missing a beat added, 'Do you know my husband died in that very bed you're sleeping in. He just sat bolt upright, went blue in the face and I knew he'd gone. Anyway, would you like another slice of toast?'

Janette: One other interesting fact about Scarborough was in 1981 Jane Leeves was one of our dancers. Although you may know Jane better as Kelsey Grammer's love interest Daphne Moon from the worldwide TV smash hit Frasier — amazing huh?

24

KENNY EVERETT

Ian: During the 1980s we would get a lot of guest slots on Blankety Blank and Summer Specials. In fact we were on what many people believe was the best ever Blankety Blank when the late Kenny Everett broke Terry Wogan's stick microphone in two.

Kenny tended to be so extravagant he took over whenever he was on, and back then we weren't confident enough to butt in, which meant we hardly got to say a word. I would dread when Everett was anything with us as he was so OTT. He got into some bizarre argument with me on screen over a tie. He kind of looked me up and down and said 'Mmm a tie - how sixties'. But then he really got my back up by saying 'Are you Scottish? Ah yes I hear you are still stuck in the sixties up there'.

Immediately I don't like this guy, which Janette could instantly sense. Frankly I wanted to knock his block off. In fact during a break in recording I followed Kenny into the toilet - he must have thought it was his lucky day - and confronted him. I said 'I don't like having the piss taken out of me on national TV - you better cool it or else'.

Kenny immediately melted and said 'Oh no darling, I was just having a laugh'. I had worked myself up into a rage at this point and slammed him up against a wall and said 'Well I didn't hear anyone laughing'.

He then apologised profusely and we returned to the studio. After that he was great with us, even gracious - I wonder why? But people like Everett really used to annoy me with their little Scottish jibes. In fact Terry Wogan was always a little bit inclined that way too. He would say 'Ah so you've come down from Scotland - this will be the first time you've seen electric lights then'. I should have followed him into the toilets too for a little chat - but he was bigger than me. I suppose if I got into the habit of following everyone into the loos who insulted us I'd never be out of the lavvy. But nothing gets a Scotsman's back up more than someone insulting their country or their accent.

Janette: We never really got to know Terry Wogan though - I don't think many people did, because he never socialised with the guests. He would leave as soon as filming finished. We used to have a lot more fun when Les Dawson took over. He was a great laugh. Ted Rogers was a lovely man too whenever we did 3-2-1. Once I came on with one of those umbrellas that fitted to your head and a water pump for rain to sing 'I'm Singing in The Rain'. Unfortunately Ted got soaked during my little sketch and all the dye in his hair ran down his face.

Ian: But showbiz egos are exceptionally fragile things. I remember once we were performing Bigger Isn't Better from The Windsor Big Top musical of Barnum for an ITV Summer Special and we really pulled out all the stops for it. We did this circus sketch, with stilt walkers where I was the Ringmaster wearing a beautiful sequined suit. We also had It's A Knockout wrestlers costumes that we wore. Anyway it looked so good that ITV used us as a promotion clip on the telly.

But Michael Crawford - who of course shot to fame as Frank Spencer before becoming a huge musical star - was apparently sitting in his dressing room at the London Palladium while starring in Windsor Big Top. He saw our trailer and it's claimed he said 'No one does Barnum but me'. He complained and we had eight minutes cut from our act. And all because Crawford didn't like a little bit of competition, sad isn't it really?

Janette: It was the first time that I wasn't just doing Jimmy on the telly, and I got to show off my tap dancing skills and a whole load of other routines, it looked great. But then this petty man, who had nothing to do with our show, put a stop to it. So I was destined to only be seen as Wee Jimmy for years to come.

Ian: His argument was that it would confuse the public having two Barnums, but how anyone could confuse The Krankies with Michael Crawford is beyond me. Unfortunately I never got to meet Mr Crawford - maybe he'd have been the next on my list for a little chat in the toilet too.

Janette: When the summer special went to air we could be seen in the finale dressed as these characters from Barnum, but no one got to see our show. I was in tears over that.

25

LENA ZAVARONI

Janette: In 1984 we met Lena Zavaroni for the first time, who was the Scottish child singer whose life would come to a terrible, tragic end when she wasted away from anorexia. She was managed by a lady called Dorothy Solomon and we did some Summer Time Specials with Lena. Her manager went everywhere with her because she was so young.

Ian: It turned out she knew my brother Alistair because he was the insurance man from her home on the Isle of Rothesay. He had said to her if you ever see Ian and Janette talk to them, so she did.

Janette: She was a lovely wee girl. We were playing in Eastbourne with her one night and were going back to London in a car laid on by ITV. I said 'You can come with us if you want'. And she seemed really excited about that, because we were company for her. But her manager Dorothy said 'No Lena, you're coming with me because Janette smokes and you've got a bad chest'. I felt sorry for her because she was so lonely. Even at that early stage I think she was showing signs of anorexia as she was getting quite thin.

There was always such a big fuss made over her food. She would never eat in the chuck wagon with the rest of us and she would always go off to eat somewhere else, that's if she did eat anything at all. She was a deeply unhappy kid, but seemed to light up when she saw us.

When we did Great Yarmouth in 1983 one day Ian decided that we should have a beach barbecue at Winston-On-Sea, which is a really quiet spot. Ian prepared all these home-made hamburgers and we arrived around one o'clock with all the dancers and musicians who came on this lovely summer's day. One of the dancers, Debbie Payne was seeing the saxophone player, but his long term girlfriend had just come over from Australia, so Debbie's nose was a bit out of joint. Anyway at one point she decided she needed a pee and the only place she could go for some privacy was into the rushes. When she came out she said 'Something's stung me?' We thought she was just trying to get some attention because she was feeling a bit down at her love rival being at the barbecue too and anyway Ian had only just started cooking the burgers. About half an hour later she started going blue in the lips.

Ian: The irony was her love rival from Australia was a nurse who became very concerned about Debbie - she hadn't a clue Debbie had been coping off with her boyfriend in her absence. She asked me if there was anything dangerous in this part of the country and I said 'Naw - you get some Adders, but not around here'. By this point Debbie starts to hallucinate, yet all the time I'm still thinking she's at it.

Janette: But this nurse found two pin prick bite marks on Debbie's leg and insisted we take her to a hospital.

Ian: I phoned the cops and asked if there were any snakes around here and they told me we shouldn't have even been on the beach at this time of year because it was breeding season for the Adders and added 'Didn't I see the signs?' There were no signs whatsoever.

Janette: We got Debbie into a car and she's been sick all the way to the hospital in a Marks & Spencers poly bag, but all the vomit was coming through the holes in the bottom. She ended up in hospital for three weeks with anaphylaxis - a severe reaction from the snake venom. The poor girl nearly died. Of course our musicians were as sensitive as ever and used to throw plastic snakes at her during visiting hours.

Ian: A local zoologist examined Debbie's bite marks in hospital and reckoned it had been a huge snake about three feet long and said it'd only attacked her because she must have stood on or near its nest - she had walked into a nest of vipers.

But it was in Great Yarmouth that year when we met a guy called Joe Terry who had a company called Magnum Concerts, who promoted people like Paul Young at the time, but wanted to break into comedy. So we went on tour with a singer, four girl dancers, The Great Soprendo and us. This guy Joe got us a tour bus and our first job was in Wick on the start of a 48 gig tour. This was no rock 'n' roll tour coach though. It was a right old rickety banger from Oldham with the catchy slogan 'Another One Of Alf's' written on the back. But we all travelled in this thing, with an articulated lorry full of lighting and speakers behind us rolling into these wee towns. Joe made a fortune because we were playing wee town halls that he'd rented for two bob and we were on the telly so they were packed out.

One of these gigs was at Greenock Town Hall which was so dilapidated that the balcony had been condemned. All we were allowed to put up there was one spotlight guy.

Before the show I nipped out to get some sandwiches and these wee boys were like 'Hey mister where's Jimmy?' They were nice wee scamps and said they couldn't afford a ticket. So I said if you keep quiet I'll allow the three of you on to the balcony to watch the show, but you mustn't say a thing. When we went on stage I glanced up and there must have been 150 kids up on the balcony, jumping around. They were swinging on the scaffolding for the lighting rigs and running riot - and all on this balcony which had been condemned. The theatre manager wasn't best pleased with me for letting them in.

We also played the Corran Hall in Oban which only had a cooker and a 13amp plug - and we were trying to bring in these huge lighting rigs. So this young techie decided to wire up his lights to the power from a street lamp. But when we put all our lights on it blew every street light in Oban. This techie crapped himself and ran out into the street to quickly undo his cable before the cops arrived. We ended up doing this show on reduced lights but it was still too much for the venue's fuse box, which kept tripping. So this techie ended up gaffer taping the trip switches down, so they couldn't flick off. All the way through our show we could hear the hum from the electric box grow louder and louder - I'm surprised he didn't burn the place down.

By this time I was complaining bitterly to the promoter about the state of the venue in Oban which didn't even have any seat numbers. But he took me aside and in a conspiratorial whisper said 'It's only cost me £47 to rent the place - and I've taken £4,000 in ticket sales. We don't pay for the electricity either even though we've used up their year's supply.' So basically I kept my mouth shut after that.

Janette and I celebrated our anniversary in Oban and we were wondering what to do. We were staying in this hotel and I decided - as was my want - to bare my arse in the restaurant. But as I turned round there was a glass annex full of OAPs staring right at me.

Janette: Even today when we meet dancers who used to work with us, they still talk about our tours and say they enjoyed some of the best days of their lives on the road with us. They're like our extended family as they all got married and stay in touch and bring their kids to our shows now, which is lovely.

The musicians and the dancers were like school boys and girls, they were always whispering about who they fancied then go away with each other. But some of them met their future husbands and wives on those tours, so no wonder they have fond memories of those times. We just seemed to laugh and laugh every day.

We repeated that 48 day tour the next year, but this time the promoter - who knew he'd make a load of money out of this by this time - gave us a proper tour bus when we went on the road for the summer of 1984. In fact it was Status Quo's tour bus and it was very luxurious with all the mod cons.

It also had loads of bunk beds and, of course, the dancers and the musicians thought this was heaven - I don't think they were ever out of those beds. They'd joke about how they'd all joined the 3ft high club.

26

IAN'S BRUSH WITH DEATH

Janette: Ian and I weren't on the tour bus that year with the 3ft high club, because Ian became very ill when he suffered a massive haemorrhage one night. That was mainly down to our lifestyle because Ian has no spleen and we really shouldn't have been hitting the booze so much. We'd also been for a big curry the night before the haemorrhage. Basically what he has is veracious veins in his oesophagus, which can be controlled through diet, which we weren't doing at the time. Even an aspirin would make them bleed. That particular night he'd got up to take paracetamol and had taken aspirin by accident. So that combined with the boozing and the curry meant we had to rush into hospital.

There was blood everywhere. He was coughing it up and passing it too. I was really frightened.

We were in the middle of the tour and were due to play Leicester, but had to cancel - something we had never done. That's how serious it was. We only had a couple days off and then fortunately he was okay. I suppose he shouldn't have gone back to work so soon but we needed to finish the tour.

After that he went to see a Harley Street specialist who used laser treatment on the veins. But they bled again in 1990 when we were in Belfast doing panto and again we were perhaps over doing things once more. Although Ian is a lot more careful these days. He never drinks spirits.

So it was just our luck that Ian fell ill when we had this incredible tour bus. But the rest of them ran riot, drinking and watching blue movies on video every night.

Ian: It was so frustrating meeting them at the venues and they'd all be coming off the bus giggling and larking around, having a wonderful time, while I felt like death warmed up.

Janette: We had a trombone player Andy Compton playing with us in Aylesbury once. They arrived outside the theatre at six in the morning, after drinking all through the night. A police horse had just left a huge big pile of shite and Andy jumped out, took his trousers down and squatted above it - everyone took photos.

Ian: It was a blessing that I wasn't on that bus because I think I would have done myself some serious damage. I knew I was drinking too much as after a gig we'd hop on the bus and drink through the night until you passed out while travelling to the next gig.

When I went to see the specialist Mr Benns, he had pictures on the wall of himself performing operations on that television show Your Life In Their Hands.

He was quite a character, and would look over the top of his little half moon specs at you. It'd be 'Ah Ian Tough from The Krankies, isn't it? Do you fancy a brandy?' Then he went 'Oh no, sorry I better not offer you anything like that in your condition'. Like I said, quite a character. Anyway, he sat and listened to me describe my symptoms while taking notes. He then went over my case file and basically said I had veracious veins in my gullet and that I'd have to have them removed.

He then asked me to tell him in all honesty, what I drink on a week to week basis. I actually told the truth, saying, 'Maybe a few beers at night, a bottle of wine with dinner and round off the evening with a few ports'. He said 'That's not bad for a week', I went 'No, no, no that's not for a week - that's every night'.

He explained that I didn't have a drink problem, but the problem was my body and my liver in particular couldn't handle that amount as my liver was doing the work of two organs as I had no spleen.

I asked him if I should quit the drink for good and he said 'Well, technically I should quit the drink for good, but I'm not going to because I enjoy it. So by all means have a few wines, have a few beers but what you should never do is binge drink', which is exactly what I'd been doing. Sometimes I'd go for four days during the week without touching a drop then the last night of a big show I'd say to everyone 'Right let's go and get bevvied'. That's apparently the worst thing anyone can do.

It's a terrible thing that it takes getting ill to give you a fright. I'm just lucky I got the warning and I'd have been an idiot to ignore it and I didn't drink for a year after that to give me time to recover. Then I started having a glass of wine or two - good stuff mind. But the older you get then the less you want to drink anyway. I was also smoking too, but I realised that with my bad bronchitis, smoking didn't really suit me, so I quit that too.

Janette: The musicians also keep in touch with us after all these years. They've always told us that they couldn't believe that they had a wilder time being on tour with the Krankies than they ever had being on tour with a rock band.

Ian: They always told us we were madder than these rock stars. They said our parties were better too because everyone laughed together and no one held court - everyone was treated the same, whereas with these rock guys, they all had massive egos and when they talked you had to listen, which doesn't sound like much fun to me.

27

DEFECTING TO ITV

Ian: We were never really aware of how successful Crackerjack! had become until we were told through the grapevine that Michael Grade - who was head of LWT at the time - had gone home and said to his children 'Turn the telly over', and they said 'No, we're watching Jimmy Krankie'.

Michael asked 'Who is Jimmy Krankie?' Then he sat down and watched the show. Well the story goes that before the credits started rolling he had called our agent Laurie Mansfield and said 'I want the Krankies for LWT - how much do you want?'

Laurie then negotiated for us £4,000 a week instead of the £600 we were getting from the BBC. Apparently Michael baulked at our demands, until he checked our viewing figures and said we'd be perfect for the ITV network on a Saturday night. I tell you there's nothing quite like being head hunted to get you a whacking big pay-rise.

Janette: ITV put us on at quarter past five on a Saturday and called it The Krankies Klub.

Ian: David Bell was the producer and he wanted the whole show to be a situation comedy.

Janette: Russell Lane was our writer, who was also writing Russ Abbot's Madhouse at the time. But to be honest, I think working on two big shows was too much for Russell and he was under severe pressure. So we went back to doing more of a variety show with pop groups. We also gave Northern Irish comic Jimmy Cricket his first regular TV spot.

Ian: We knew Jimmy from years ago and so when the producer asked if we minded Jimmy getting his own slot, we said 'Not at all'.

Janette: That was during the first year at LWT, for the second year Bobby Davro got a slot on the show, which proved to be his big break. But that was the last series we did with LWT. I felt it wasn't working because they were trying to make it more adult than Crackerjack!. I just didn't think the scripts were that great and they wouldn't allow us any input whatsoever.

Ian: We just knew the show wasn't as good as it had been on the BBC - it certainly wasn't good enough for 5.15pm on a Saturday night.

Janette: The BBC had just spent a fortune buying in The Dukes Of Hazzard, but The Krankies Klub still managed to trounce them in the ratings by 2 to1.

Ian: We were still getting between eight and nine million viewers, but that wasn't good enough for ITV who were looking for 18 million viewers. But regardless those figures seemed to be good enough for the BBC who thought they better rehire us, which was a godsend - although we never told them that.

Janette: The same scenario happened to Morecambe and Wise before us, who had moved to ITV, which proved to be an unsuccessful switch, and then returned to the BBC.

Ian: Funnily enough at that point Michael Grade moved from LWT to the BBC too. So after two seasons and two Christmas specials for LWT it was back to Woodlane - and they even gave us more money, with our wages going up to £4,500 a week.

Janette: Although you must remember that that was only for the six weeks of filming - it wasn't £4,500 a week for a year. But it was still a lot better than the £300 each they used to pay us. Although the BBC did insist that we had a year long sabbatical from national television when we switched sides again. So in the meantime we did The Joke Machine, which was a regional show for Borders TV, so we didn't return to the BBC until 1985.

Ian: But the back up the BBC gave us this time around was second to none. They moved us to quarter to six on a Saturday night, called it The Krankies Elektronik Komic and shot the whole show on film, which meant it looked quality. They also got us to do location shoots, which meant getting us out and about more. We made mini sitcoms for the show like Mayhem On The Overland Express - a mickey take of Murder On The Orient Express - and Jimmy-Burgermac, a send up of John Nettles's hugely popular cop series Bergerac.

Janette: It was great working with the producer Paul Cianni again as he made everything fun.

Ian: The main difference I noticed was that LWT was very luvvie, although at the aftershow they'd have a spread on you would struggle to see at a Golden Wedding Anniversary, it was incredible. Back at the BBC it was just canteen food, although the quality on screen increased ten fold. Even our titles on screen were far superior to LWT's.

Janette: Our sketches were excellent too - good, cheeky wee plays and I loved doing them. We had two writers, including Morecombe and Wise's script writer Sid Green. The only downside was that all Sid was doing was revamping old Morecombe and Wise scripts and giving them to us. He didn't even try to disguise it very well. He would simply Tippex over the names on the script, but would forget to do even that after the fourth page.

Ian: So you'd be reading 'Ian says, Jeanette says', then it'd slip into 'Eric says, Ernie says'. I'd ask 'Hey Sid, am I Ernie in this one or Eric?'

Janette: We didn't get on with Sid at all. He really wasn't a very nice person. His material simply didn't suit us and frankly we didn't really want Morecambe and Wise rejects. It was insulting.

Ian: I met a comic Bryan Marshall in the lifts one day, who I'd known for years. My mind was preoccupied as I was deeply worried about one of Sid's sketches. I had just been given a bollocking by Sid after I raised my doubts about it and he had told me it was my job to find the laughs and make it funny. He actually reduced Janette to tears that day, as we said, not a very nice man at all.

Anyway I went off to the pub with Bryan to drown my sorrows and as it turned out he was doing a bit of writing, so that afternoon he wrote me a sketch called Toni Macaroni's Café.

Janette: Bryan had a young family and he knew what tickled his sons, instead of Sid Green who was living in yesteryear. So we told our director 'We want Bryan' and we got him.

Ian: We had people like Kevin Keegan guest starring and coming into Toni Macaroni's Café to be served by Wee Jimmy. We also had people on like Bananarama, Lisa Stansfield, Shakin' Stevens and Slade but we'd never really meet the bands as they'd record on a different days, although we did go to the famous Stringfellows Club with Keegan after filming and he was great fun.

Janette: We also had a great budget of £80,000 a week for The Elektronik Komic and they made sure they spent every penny. If Ian needed a jumper the wardrobe people would go to Saville Row to get one.

Ian: They'd spend £300 on a bloody jumper in the mid-80s. I didn't even want to wear the stuff, but they had to make sure they used up all the budget or they wouldn't get more next year.

Janette: That's why they took the cast and crew out on location shoots too. One sketch we did was with The Great Soprendo, played by Geoffrey Durham who was married to Victoria Wood for years. Victoria came over to Guernsey for a week while we were filming Burger-Mac. The Guernsey tourist board took us all out one day as a thank you for filming on their patch. We had to meet all these pain in the arse councillors at a meal and swap seats after every course so they could get to speak to the whole lot of us.

Ian: Anyway one of them said to Victoria - who wasn't really a well known name at the time - 'My, I bet your husband keeps you amused all the time with his tricks'. Victoria feigned interest and said 'Oh yes, I'm always laughing', then this plonker said to her 'I bet you're the happiest little housewife around'. How to win friends eh?

Janette: We were so bored with all these stupid councillors that we made our excuses to leave saying that we had to get up early tomorrow for filming. As soon as we left the restaurant and turned a corner, Ian, Victoria, Geoffrey and I all started dancing a jig in the carpark - only to realise that all these bloody councillors had followed us out and were right behind us.

I worked years later with Victoria when I did an episode of Dinner Ladies with Julie Walters, where I played an old Scottish bag woman. It can be strange meeting someone you knew at the start of their career and you always try to see if they've changed. In my opinion Victoria had changed. She was a very astute business woman and I think she uses that hard business edge to cover up her shyness. She had progressed, but was also pretty straight. A nice woman but no edge to her. I don't think she'd have done all those daft things Ian and I got up to. Geoffrey used to always have a great laugh with us though. In 1986, we were doing Sunday in Blackpool and a Tuesday and Wednesday in Great Yarmouth and had our own tour bus to travel between the venues.

Geoffrey was huge in those days and we'd go buy wine and snacks for the bus trip, but he would buy a whole chicken, saying 'Just in case we don't get our lunch'. He would eat the chicken by himself, then we'd stop for lunch and he'd eat again.

But one night he fell asleep on the bus and Ian wrote on his forehead 'I am a cunt.' Geoffrey was none the wiser when he went to check-in at the hotel reception.

Ian: The receptionist handed over his key in silence, but when he got into the lift he saw the mirror and just burst out laughing. After that nobody would go to sleep on the bus in case we got them. If you did have 40 winks, you did it with one eye open.

Although this time around on television we had to make two shows a week and because of that we were cramming too much in and I felt the quality suffered because of it.

Janette: I disagree. I thought the quality was fine, but I do agree we were cramming too much in. It was a lot of work which eventually got to me because I came down with shingles. We had so much to learn for each show that I was obviously under pressure and my body took the brunt of that.

Ian: I think we also accepted certain sketches we wouldn't have done if we had had more time. We never had the luxury of picking and choosing.

Janette: When that series finished we went straight back to Guernsey to recover.

Ian: But do you know how they finish with you at the BBC? The only hint you are given that things are over is when you don't get invited to the BBC Christmas party. Stanley Baxter insists to this day that he still hasn't officially been told he's finished at the BBC. No one will face you, but you start to notice that certain people begin to avoid you. This happened just after we'd finished the third series and we were looking to see if anyone was going to commission the next one. We needed to know so we could organise our diary for the year - if we're taking a summer season etc. But the only thing we were told was 'Go and do your pantomime, come back and we'll have an answer for you.' Of course, as I've said, our invites for the party obviously were lost in the post so we knew something was afoot.

Again there had been another shift in styles at the BBC. For starters they were cutting down on the high budget shows like ours and also seemed to have gone off using girl dancers and orchestras. Despite all that, they did commission one last series of Krankies Elektronik Komik in 1988, before they discovered it was easier and cheaper to make more quiz shows.

Janette: We were probably suffering from a bit of over exposure at that time too. For example one Saturday night The Elektronik Komic was on, then we were on Blankety Blank AND 3-2-1.

Ian: We thought it was great at the time, not knowing that people would get sick of the sight of us. Also all these other shows insisted Janette appeared as Jimmy, even though our stage act was much more than that. So basically Jimmy was everywhere - eventually even I got sick and tired of switching on the telly only to discover we were on again.

Janette: It wasn't a problem for me, because I've always enjoyed playing Jimmy. I'm not one of these performers who grows to resent the very thing that made them famous. Away from TV I wasn't just playing Jimmy doing the summer shows and would get a shot at something else. I always liked it when afterwards people would say to me 'Wow, I didn't know you could play such and such'. But then others would come up to me after our live performances and say 'I liked you best when you played the wee boy'.

But I can completely understand why they only wanted Jimmy on TV because anything else would have confused the children. Many, many children had no idea I was a woman - even though I was credited as Janette Tough at the end.

When I was doing Crackerjack! I wasn't allowed to sign autographs dressed as anything but Jimmy, because they wanted to keep the illusion going. Once I did it out of costume and the kids said to me 'Where's Jimmy?' and I said 'Well, I'm his sister, I'll sign an autograph for you', but they didn't like that so I always stuck to being Jimmy during Crackerjack!.

28

THE KRAZY LONDON YEARS

Janette: When we returned to the BBC we decided to buy a place in London, because we were spending £500 a week on hotels.

Ian: We got a flat for £32,000 at Oxford and Cambridge Mansions on Marylebone Road which was a fortune then, but it was just half a mile from Marble Arch - god knows what it'd be worth now.

Janette: We told Stu Francis about our wee flat and he said 'Can I come and stay with you?' We explained it was only a one bedroom flat but he didn't mind sleeping on our couch. We thought it'd be ideal to rehearse our scripts at night, but we never once bothered our backsides doing any of that stuff as we usually went to the pub. Stu was a great guest though and would bring us a cuppa tea every morning in bed, usually singing along to the radio.

We continued to travel a lot during that time because we were still working the cabaret clubs. One night we were playing in Windsor and Stu, who would normally come along with us for a drink, decided on this night he was going to bed early and asked us politely not to disturb him when we came in at one in the morning. Of course it was typical of Stu to get bored with the idea of an early night, so he went to the pub as usual and got back to the flat at about one in the morning when he decided he'd give us a surprise. He thought he'd heard us pull up outside, stripped to his underpants, tiptoed out into the street and hid behind a post box - but the door to the flat slammed shut behind him, leaving him locked outside on a bitter cold night in the middle of November. Of course it wasn't us he'd heard at all, so he was locked outside in the freezing cold for about 25 minutes until we arrived back.

Ian: He's so cold by this point that he's sobered up and realised that his big surprise wasn't such a good idea after all.

Janette: Another night we were driving back from Stringfellows in Stu's Roller and I was in the front and Ian was in the back with his feet resting between the driver and passenger seat. Ian started saying 'Look at my new Italian shoes Stu, aren't they class? They cost me a fortune'. Quick as a flash Stu put down his electric window, grabbed one of Ian's shoes and threw it onto Marylebone Road.

Ian: It was the wee small hours and there was hardly any traffic around - until just at that precise moment a big articulated lorry turned the corner and ran right over my shoe. Stu was bent over with laughter and I'm in the back wondering 'What the hell will I do with one shoe?'

Janette: We didn't really go in for the celebrity haunts, except Stringfellows where we always went after filming on a Tuesday. We'd also go to Morton's Wine Bar on a regular basis but that was only because Jim Davidson usually hung about there.

Ian: We got on very well with Peter Stringfellow because we'd used to work at his dad's club in Leeds, so he was always very good to us and insisted on sending a bottle of Dom Perignon over to our table anytime we were in.

Janette: We always brought plenty of business with us

though because whoever had been on the show, like Bryan Robson or Kevin Keegan, would join us for a drink and Stringy naturally loved having big names like that in his club.

Ian: I remember one night we went to Stringfellows with Les Dawson, who had just been to visit his wife who was ill in hospital. The place was teaming with press snapping everyone because they had a tip that Prince Edward was in there too, which was nonsense. Les was cuddling the Water Rat's secretary, who was sitting on his lap. There was honestly nothing sleazy or sexual about it, it was just the way Les was with people. He'd be doing his act saying 'Give us a kiss then', puckering up his lips the way he did on the telly. Anyway, one of the press photographers spotted him and caught him with this young thing on his lap, while Les's wife was in hospital - it would have undoubtedly made the front page.

Les beckoned the snapper over on the pretence he was going to pose for more shots. Instead he grabbed the guy's camera from around his neck, opened the back and took out his film and said 'Next time, bloody ask me first'. The photographer was nearly crying. His big exclusive had just been destroyed in front of him.

Janette: On one night out with Stu, there was this big theatre impresario who lived off Regent's Park. He took a bit of a shine to me and would say 'I love little women'. His wife had a wee crush on Stu, although it was only flirtation and nothing ever happened about it. This impresario was a heavy smoker, but never flicked his ash which always spilled down his suit. Every time you saw him he'd have a trail of ash down the front of his expensive suits.

One night they invited us all back to his place and he asked Stu to put some music on. His wife then helps Stu pick a record and she starts touching his arse. Meanwhile this impresario has got his arm around me and their Chihuahua was shagging Ian's leg - some orgy eh?

Ian: Although it all came to an abrupt halt when I punted the Chihuahua the full length of the room.

Janette: We quickly left the flat to go back to our place at Oxford and Cambridge Mansions, insisting we would wait outside for a taxi even though it was bloody freezing. It was a beautiful building, which was all floodlit with a fountain in the grounds. But just as the taxi is pulling up Stu pushes Ian into the fountain.

Ian: I was soaked through with freezing water. I shouted at Stu 'What the hell did you go and do that for?' And he said 'Because you were going to do it to me ya bastard'. And he was right. He must have caught that mischievous look in my eye and hit me with a pre-emptive attack. He was always up to crazy things like that.

Janette: Stu was a keep-fit fanatic and used to go running into work every morning wearing a nylon suit. He thought this meant he could go boozing every night to the wee small hours because he'd be able to sweat it out.

Ian: We did a trick on Stu though because he was always complaining that he didn't get many fan letters, especially from girls. So I wrote him this letter saying 'Dear Stu, I have been a fan of yours since I was a little girl. I am now 23 years of age and if I say so myself, I am quite a pretty girl. I will be in your neck of the woods and wonder if you would consider meeting for a drink and maybe even escort me to my hotel room (I wish! I wish!), yours etc etc'.

Stu burst into our dressing room waving my letter around frantically saying 'Look at this - a bird and she sounds hot'. I'm playing it dead cool saying 'Are you sure it's for real?' And Stu's like 'Of course it's for real just look at the writing and what's she's saying'. So the night he was getting all dressed up to meet her I thought I've taken this too far and told him - and he called me all the names under the sun.

Anyway about a week later, we were coming off the stage at

Paignton Festival Theatre at the end of the show. But while we'd been performing Stu had been out for a walk and met a a tramp. Apparently this guy said 'You're Stu Francis from Crackerjack!. I've always wanted to meet you'. And Stu said, 'Funnily enough Ian Krankie has always wanted to meet you - he's heard you've got lots of jokes and he'd like to hear them'. Stu took this tramp into my dressing room, sat him down and left. So when we went into our room we didn't know what to think of this nice big guy - who I knew obviously wasn't the full shilling when he said 'Stu Francis said you wanted to hear some of my jokes'. I thought 'The bastard's got me back'. This guy then started telling us all these awful jokes and of course we had to listen to them. We couldn't exactly chuck him out. All I could hear from the corridor outside was Stu killing himself laughing. He had well and truly wreaked his revenge.

Janette: Stu was always a brilliant practical joker, but he's also a dear pal. A truly brilliant person.

We were very close to him and his family and did a lot of summer seasons with him. We watched his kids grow up. His daughter Zoë was just three when we started Crackerjack! and she used to always quiz me in the canteen about Jimmy, asking if Wee Jimmy was really a mummy - because she knew I was Jimmy and knew I was a woman, she just wasn't too sure how it all worked out.

29

THE AXE FALLS

Ian: After we didn't get an invite to the BBC Christmas party in 1988 I decided to take the bull by the horns and phoned up Harry King at Border TV, who we'd done Joke Machine with. He was immediately interested, so Janette and I went up there and negotiated the contract ourselves and created KTV. This time we didn't have a studio audience, which meant we could just work on camera and also - as we do in the theatre - we could ad-lib. We filmed it in the borders, up in Dumfries and Galloway and had a great time as it seemed like the pressure was suddenly off us and we could relax and do what we wanted to do. We never heard from the BBC again.

The only positive point we took from our departure was that the BBC didn't replace us with someone else, which meant it wasn't us they didn't want, it was just the end of that style of variety entertainment - for better or for worse. I hope I don't come across as being bitter about the whole situation because I'm honestly not. That's just showbiz and in the end everything must change.

Janette: After us the BBC got rid of Russ Abbot, then Little and Large and we were all replaced by game shows. It didn't bother me because I'm such an easy come, easy go, type of person - but Russ Abbot and Little and Large were extremely popular shows that the whole family would sit down to watch, so it just seemed daft to get rid of them. They had the ratings that today's Saturday night shows can only dream about.

But that was then and you can't worry about it because television gets rid of everyone in the end.

However Ian and I had a ball doing KTV, which was also networked. It was exactly the sort of telly we had always wanted to do and it was an extremely popular show with huge figures of five and a half million viewers at quarter past four on a Monday afternoon.

We had great guests too like the actress Patty Combs, Bob Holness, Magnus Magnusson and Nick Owen because whatever shows they were doing we always did a send-up of them.

Ian: The sketch with the newsreader Nick Owen, was hysterical. We filmed it at Carlisle races and tried to convince Nick that our pantomime horse would win - Carlisle even held up that day's race meeting so we could film our scenes.

Janette: We did 21 episodes of KTV over three years. It was undoubtedly our best years in television.

Ian: Then the big chop came - political correctness struck and we were out on our ear. They were asking us to explain, 'What is the relationship between this wee boy and the man? And they're a married couple in real-life - this isn't right at all'.

Well, I don't believe any of our viewers looked at us in that light. We came from a much simpler era. I mean no one used to bat an eyelid when Morecombe and Wise used to share a bed on screen - now they'd be branded a couple of old queens. Incredible isn't it? To me the people who see something sordid in our act are the sordid ones themselves - because they're thinking about it in the first place.

The change happened when Margaret Thatcher put the ITV contracts out to tender and Border lost theirs and were swept up by Granada who in turn had to get approval for our series KTV from a new Children's Board. This board consisted of a minister, a priest, a psychologist, an ordinary housewife and a TV director.

Well our act obviously set alarm bells ringing in their meetings and that's when we were deemed sleazy or tacky or whatever. We'd gone from having millions of viewers to suddenly be out on our arses and all because six anonymous people decided there was something unsavoury about our show.

That's why they've ended up with so many cartoons for children, because as far as they're concerned, it's safe.

So in 1991 that was the end of The Krankies as far television was concerned.

Janette: I was sad it all ended, but I get over these things very quickly. And anyway we were getting older at that point. You can get away with an awful lot on stage when you are getting on a bit, but the cameras never lie. I would ask the director not to come in too close with the camera because quite simply Wee Jimmy was getting a bit wrinkly around the edges.

Ian: We were up against a brick wall with television and there was nowhere left for us to go. It was the same for all the old variety acts. Cannon and Ball couldn't get on television if they murdered someone. Janette and I were in our 40s by this point and we had no choice but to turn our back on Children's TV and concentrate on the cabaret circuit again.

But even that proved to be tough because we were struggling to get audiences on the cabaret circuit after being Children's TV stars. Adults didn't want to turn up to watch a couple of kiddie's telly entertainers.

Janette: It was fine during panto and summer seasons, but you couldn't convince cabaret punters to come and see us. That's really when we became the butt of everyone's joke because the new audiences only saw us as hasbeen children's entertainers - so from primetime TV we became the pay off line for everyone's act.

There's hardly a day goes by when we're not watching the TV and hear our name used. Tony Blackburn even said the Scottish comic Rhona Cameron looked like me before he won ITV's first I'm A Celebrity...Get Me Out Of Here in the summer of 2002. But as I've always said to Ian, these people are doing us a great favour, because at least they are mentioning us. That means our name is still getting banded around, however derogatory it's used.

Ian: It's really nice when people come up to us and say 'Why are you two not still on the telly - there's so much rubbish on'. That happens nearly every day, whether it's just something to get a conversation going I don't know. But it seems strange that what's on the telly now seems to be the first thing folk want to talk to us about.

Janette: Our agent Laurie Mansfield was never concerned when telly finished with us. He always used to say 'There are people who will come and go but The Krankies will NEVER be forgotten'.

Ian: I won't pretend that the chop didn't devastate me though. Janette handled it a lot better than I did.

Janette: I've always liked live work better than TV anyway. So I just said to Ian 'Oh forget it, let's go back to what we love best'. So we'd do the summer seasons and panto and would go to Australia for a few months too. I loved it.

30

THE DEATH OF JANETTE'S PARENTS

Janette: It's incredible how things work out though because at the time we were finishing our last KTV show for Borders in 1991 my mother took seriously ill and was diagnosed with bowel cancer. But because we were working at Newcastle in panto with Anita Dobson, it was quite easy for me to commute up and down to see her.

But by the time the panto finished my mum was really poorly and Ian and I moved back to Scotland to be with her. We stayed in my parents' old house in Queenzieburn with my dad until my mum passed away at the age of 76 in April. 1991. My father by this time was 80 and because I was an only child, they had no one else to look after them so it was my duty, and my honour, to be there for them both.

The people in Queenzieburn were fantastic and would do anything to help. I remember Ian's Jaguar would be parked outside my parent's house and the kids passing by on their way to school would say 'Don't touch that motor - it's Jimmy Krankies'. A wee boy even asked me 'Jimmy have ye come home to look after yer mammy?' They were so nice and warm to me when I needed it the most. It felt good to be back home.

Of course it didn't take long before some journalists started snooping around - well it was pretty obvious where we were staying with this flash motor sitting outside a wee council house in Queenzieburn. One female reporter rang my parents one day and said to me, 'I understand you've given up work to come home and nurse your mother'. I said 'That's right'. She then asked if she could do an interview with me and I said 'No', because for a start my mother didn't know she had cancer.

What this reporter said next I will never forget. She asked me 'Well, when your mother dies can I come and interview you?' I burst into a flood of tears and hung up. I have never heard anything so insensitive in all my life. I don't have a big downer on journalists at all, even though many of them have written some pretty nasty things about us in the past. But I just wish they would just take a second to stop and think. I wasn't some faceless 'Children's TV star', she was talking to. I was just a daughter who didn't want her mammy to die.

We took the decision not to tell my mum she had cancer under advice from the specialist. He had told us her bowel cancer had spread to her liver but after an operation to remove some of it and insert a colostomy bag she would maybe have eight months left to live. After the operation I asked if she would feel okay for a while and the doctor said she would. It was a heartbreaking decision but I didn't want the time my mum had left to be constantly worrying about cancer.

It seemed to work because after her operation she really picked up and felt quite well for three months out of the 10 she ended up living for. I don't think she would have had that three months grace if she had been told what was really wrong with her. She would have constantly been worrying about what was to come. So it was a heart-breaking decision, but I think we made the right choice in the end. The thing is my mum wasn't daft, she knew she was dying, but we never discussed the word cancer with her and I think that's the way she liked it.

My mum was a wonderful patient and fortunately was only in hospital for the last five days of her life. Along with my father and Ian, we all really helped her get through those months. She was in pain and on morphine, but never complained. Unfortunately as the morphine doses increased her personality changed and she started to wander around in a bit of a daze, thinking that no one liked her. But all you could do was take her hand and assure her she was okay. I still miss my mum.

We went back to Guernsey after the funeral and I wanted to take my dad with us, but he wanted to get things tied up with his house. That's probably when those 10 hard months really took their toll on me. I had to leave my dad at home by himself for the first time in over 60 years. It broke my heart.

It's horrible how bad things all come along at once, with TV finishing then my mum dying and it left Ian and I feeling pretty low. My father came to Guernsey and he loved being there and coming out on the boat with us. One day Ian said 'How'd you like to sail over to France with us Bill', and he was so excited. He was out helping us get through the locks and everything, which worried me sick because I knew he was bad with angina - but he loved it. He used to say to me 'Janette, sailing is just like posh caravaning'. He was in seventh heaven. We even took him to Spain on holiday where we rented a villa. He'd never really been abroad before and he found it fascinating. He would also join us while we were on tour.

So when we did a summer season at the Gaiety in Ayr, he'd come down to Ayr for three weeks. And when we did Wolverhampton panto at the end of 1991, he came down there for a month too. It gave him a new lease of life.

But after he came to stay with us in Blackpool in 1992 for a month, he went back home in August and had a stroke. So we'd come up every Sunday to visit him in Stobhill Hospital in Glasgow before driving back down to Blackpool. While he was in hospital recovering from his stroke the doctor also discovered he had blood cancer, so we knew he didn't have long to go. When he left the hospital we had him sell his house and come to live with us. Although he was ill he still came everywhere with us, including panto in Hull and then the following year, to Scarborough for the summer season. All our dancers would make a fuss of him as he was such a nice man.

He actually died in Scarborough in 1993 while we were working there. He was so ill by that point he was having blood transfusions and would fall over all the time. It was a dreadful shame.

We had three shows a week to put on and rehearse and during that time we had to put my dad into a nursing home in Bournemouth. It was a beautiful home though, more like a five star hotel and my dad loved it. Unfortunately he was so ill he kept going between the home and hospital before he passed away three weeks later. He was cremated on June 28, 1993, on his 83rd birthday - so he went out on the same day he came in. He would have liked the irony.

This sounds terrible, but my father's death was like a relief in a way. A relief for both him and for me. I'm just glad I got to spend so much time with both my parents in the end. I hadn't lived with them since I was 18, and stayed miles away from them. I'd only see them about four times a year, so it was beautiful getting to know them once more.

In truth though I don't think they would have ever wanted me to have been one of those daughters who stayed at home. I was a little girl from a mining village who ended up living in London and Guernsey and was on the telly and working in the theatre, which I loved. They wanted me to live a life and I certainly have done that. Had we been contracted to TV at that point I probably wouldn't have been able to look after them the way we did. So being dropped from the telly was a blessing in disguise.

But I felt really sorry for Ian. I mean that sort of situation really tests your marriage when you are dragging an ill parent around with you at both work and home, but we got through it and he never once complained.

Ian: We were at a crossroads in our lives anyway, deciding what to do next, so it's funny how it all works out, where we ended up with more time on our hands just as Janette's parents needed us the most. Career wise though, I was worried, but not too worried because we still had the summer seasons and the panto. I coped by renting an office in St Enoch's Square right in the middle of Glasgow and I used to go there every morning at 10am and come back at four in the afternoon. I would spend the day on the phone, calling our bookers, musicians, checking on costumes, the whole bit. That gave me some space and kept me working so we weren't tripping over each other in Janette's parents' house while her mother was ill.

Janette: After my parents passed, our years became divided into four sections. There was the summer section, the panto season, the time of year after Christmas when no one gets any work anyway, so we go off to Australia to play a lot of golf and enjoy the good weather, then we would return home or work the cruise ships. It was a very nice lifestyle without having to think 'Oh God, I wonder if we'll be on telly again?' That's all stress. We also worked a lot better together when we didn't have any of that stress. And if we don't have any work on, we didn't care as we never had a family to support, it's only us two. No hassle at all - our life is our own.

Ian: Although there was a really dull spell after that time where we had some pretty shitty jobs and saw a side of the business that we really didn't care for. We were also working our way down the bill which was hard to take, but you had to accept it. For example at Blackpool in Summer of 1992 we were the support to Bobby Davro - who of course got his break on our TV show. Funny old world isn't it?

Janette: I didn't care that we were now the support act once again. As I said it meant the pressure was off and we'd be finished by the first half then it was off to a restaurant or home. Bobby actually was suffering more than us as he'd just lost his TV variety show too and was deeply unhappy in his personal life so he wasn't firing on all cylinders. He was going out with this girl Zoë Nicholas for a long time, who was in his show. But he wanted to finish it with her and his dressing room door was always shut and he didn't talk to us much.

Ian: That was strange as we'd not only given him his start but had toured with him several times before, but I don't think he was happy with himself at that point in time.

Janette: Since then he's been great with us again so he was obviously just going through a bad time.

Ian: However, we had a superb season at The Grand in Blackpool which is a fantastic venue and we really packed them in. And all we did was 17 minutes in the show then we would play a round of golf or relax at our rented cottage, which was on the grounds of this big estate owned by two gay guys who had done an amazing job of doing it up. So we had the run of 12 acres where you could see deer and even llamas wandering free.

Janette: There was a big swimming pool which we used all the time. It was very tranquil, very relaxing and just perfect - and we got to enjoy all that for working just 17 minutes a day.

The manager of the Grand, Paul Isles was then hired to run the new Festival Theatre in Edinburgh and he said to us on the last night that when he opened in Edinburgh he wanted to stage the biggest variety show seen in Scotland in years - and he wanted us to close the bill.

He really did seem to be taken with us. Unfortunately for him the chattering classes in Edinburgh didn't like his idea of bringing The Krankies to town and they slaughtered him in the press. Even a local Councillor called Nolan went ballistic about it. He was on TV and said 'The Krankies were only fit for back-street concerts in Craigmillar', which was a bit harsh on the people of Craigmillar.

Ian: We were flooded with calls from the media including The Scotsman and STV all wanting our comments, which we gladly gave.

Janette: Nolan came out with some more classic quotes. He said that the Festival Theatre shouldn't be opened with a Variety Show, it should be The Three Tenors - well you would need more than three tenners to see Domingo and his mates compared to the £12 we were charging.

Ian: When we finished the show, I apologised to the audience that the Three Tenors couldn't make it tonight. because they were playing Craigmillar's Miners Welfare Club - the place erupted in hysterics.

Janette: The next morning we were driving back to Guernsey and there was a phone-in on some radio show and Councillor Nolan was in the studio and we were also taking part on our mobile phone. Nolan said to us 'I never watched you last night, but I heard if it had not been for me you wouldn't have had any material for your act'. I just said 'I know Councillor Nolan, it amazes us just how we've managed to survive in this business for so long without you'.

31

THE KRANKIES KRAZY STALKER

Janette: In 1990 we were at The Theatre Royal in Newcastle where we topped the bill in Aladdin with Anita Dobson and Bernard Bresslaw from the Carry On films.

One night I came out of the stage door with Anita to find what we thought was a child waiting on her own for an autograph. I spoke to her and realised it was a small woman in her twenties.

She seemed infatuated with us and asked where Ian had gone, no surprise to know he'd nipped off to the pub across the road with Bernard and our director Russell Lane. She told me she didn't have anywhere to stay and started shaking and crying and working herself up into a pretty distressed state. It turned out just before I met her, she had asked the stage doorman where we lived but he wouldn't tell her and that's when she began to get upset.

So I took her to the police station and by this time I'd suspected that this girl was not quite right and seemed to have the mind of someone a lot younger than her age. The police contacted her parents in Derby and they came up and collected her the next day.

We thought no more of it until she turned up the next year at the panto in Wolverhampton. She would wait outside the stage door almost every night, so I got a hold of her mother's phone number and told her where her daughter was. Her mum was very apologetic and I'd phone them every time their daughter was outside the stage door. They would always come and get her and take her back home, but a few nights later she'd always be back waiting for Ian and I.

But her behaviour was starting to get more and more disturbing. One time she was found walking along the motorway by the police and when she talked to me she seemed very interested in how I, being small like herself, had managed to marry Ian. Then she wanted to know why I was on stage and, more to the point, why she wasn't?

She then appeared at Blackpool that summer, staying outside the stage door for two solid weeks, asking if she could come into our dressing room. I would tell her 'No', and that she should really be back at home with her mother, because she'd be worried sick. That's when she started getting rather nasty and began writing me very disturbing letters saying she was in love with Ian and was going to kill me.

Ian: These letters had gone beyond a joke. Janette had been nothing but nice to this girl, but now she was deeply distressing Janette. I phoned the girl's parents again who told us again their daughter had had a fixation with us since she was very young. They were at their wits end themselves and had obviously been through the wringer with their daughter, but they promised they would collect her and take her to a doctor.

But it still didn't stop there and for our next shows at The New Theatre in Hull she turned up again. I had anticipated it this time and warned the theatre staff that this girl may turn up and ask for our personal details as she was harassing Janette. I showed the letters she had been writing to Janette to the theatre's management and told them to look out for her.

Sure enough she turned up once again, saying to the theatre staff that she had nowhere to stay but Janette would look after her. This time the theatre phoned her mother and the police.

But somehow this girl had got into the auditorium after our matinee performance and threatened to jump off the circle if she wasn't allowed to marry me, or something like that. The police talked her down and the theatre manager phoned her mum and dad to come and collect her, but as the manager was putting her into their car, she jumped out as they were just driving off. The police later caught her and told the parents that she would be certified if they didn't seek urgent medical help for their daughter themselves.

Again we thought we'd heard the last of it, but oh no, if anything this girl was very persistent. The following summer in Scarborough she turned up once more, but with a change of tact, saying she had come to apologise as she had been in a hospital to have treatment to get over her infatuation with Janette and me. But no sooner had she apologised, she started to tell Janette that she should let me marry her. I thought 'Well that was a waste of a year's worth of therapy.'

Janette had come to the end of her tether. It had been going on for over two years. I wouldn't say we lived in fear, but every time you came out of a show you were expecting this girl to be there and she usually was. With someone that unstable you just never know what they are going to do. She had already threatened to kill Janette so she'd obviously fantasised of doing something nasty to her, just so she could marry me.

On this occasion Janette just snapped and told the girl to get lost. She then marched back inside the theatre and called the police, told them the story and this time they arrived with a doctor who certified the girl on the spot. It's sad that it had to end like that, but she left us with little choice. Someone like that begins to cast a shadow over your life and, if you're not careful, they can end up taking over.

The last thing we ever heard from her was a letter she sent to us, saying that she'd never bother us again, as she'd once talked to Ken Dodd in Blackpool and was going to follow him from now on instead. We thought 'Good luck Ken.'

Janette: But you can imagine our hearts were in our mouths when we read in May 2003 how Ken Dodd and his girlfriend had been subjected to years of threatening behaviour from one of Ken's obsessed fans. The court case had said that this girl thought Ken's girlfriend was standing in the way of a relationship with him - it had all the hallmarks of my stalker. Incredibly, it turned out to be a different girl. So, who knows, Ken may have ended up with our stalker and this other one. Poor guy. But I dread to think what would have happened if it had carried on because obviously in Ken's case, things can get extremely out of hand and what starts as something that's just slightly annoying can escalate into something that takes over your life.

32

THE QE2

Janette: We were in Perth, Western Australia working at the time when we were approached by Cunard asking if we'd take a stint on QE2 in May of 1994, travelling from Southampton to the Mediterranean. We'd hadn't worked on any ships since the Orianna years before and being the prestigious QE2, we naturally jumped at the chance.

But as we were queuing up to get on board with the rest of the passengers behind us in the queue were two old ladies from Edinburgh. One of them then said out loud 'What are you two doing here?' I was going to ignore them, as I could tell from her tone of voice she wasn't even trying to be polite, but instead I turned round, smiled and said 'We're the cabaret for this cruise.' Well she looked as if I'd just shat in her handbag. Both their jaws dropped to the floor and they shouted in unison 'YOU'RE the cabaret - on the QE2?' I said 'Who were you expecting - Shirley bleeding Bassey?' And with that they marched off, shaking their heads and muttering to each other, something probably along the lines about how standards on the QE2 have really dropped since the last time they were onboard.

Ian: The thing is we will talk to anybody, but we'd scared off these two old snobs just by our sheer presence. The next day I got chatting to the first engineer who, it turned out, had been at school with me in Clydebank. He then told us that the night before these two old dears had been sitting at the Captain's table and when he asked them if they had been enjoying the cruise and they replied 'Oh it's marvellous, this is our fifth trip - but we were rather shocked to see that you had Glasgow comedians onboard. I mean what has the QE2 come to, using Glasgow comedians?' The captain then asked 'Well, have you been to see them?', and their reply summed it up when one of them said 'Oh no, we're not ones for laughing'. But it's nice to see that the old Glasgow/Edinburgh rivalry is still going strong.

Janette: Jack Tinker, who'd been the Daily Mail's showbiz critic for years, was also onboard this trip along with the comic Jim Bowen and we all instantly hit it off. Jim told us some great stories, including one about two Scots contestants he once had on his TV show Bullseye. These two guys had won everything on the show, from the boat to the caravan and had gone on a bender to celebrate. Eventually they passed out drunk in the hotel where Bullseye had put them up. But one of them had got up for a shit during the night and hadn't quite made it to the toilet and had crapped in a corner of the hotel bedroom instead. This contestant decided to try and get rid of the mess and seemed to remember seeing a Hoover down the corridor. So he nipped down, got the Hoover and ran it over his pile of crap. Unfortunately it wasn't actually a Hoover - it was a floor polisher and it sent the shit spraying over every wall in the room.

Ian: Jim was a great laugh and every night we'd sit in the bar swapping stories.

Janette: However, just a few days into the trip we were hit with this awful storm. It was getting pretty violent around midnight as we were all sitting in the bar together. Then I noticed a really old woman with a zimmer frame trying to make her way along to her cabin. I got lumbered with her as all the staff are quite fly and when they see an old doddery person, they're experts at making themselves scarce. It took me ages to take her along to her cabin. It was getting really rough at this point and as we made our painfully slow way through a dining room all the crockery was smashing on the ground. The woman kept saying 'I'm going to be sick', but I managed to coax her along and eventually got to her room.

By the time I came back it seemed like I'd been away for hours, and I told Jim and Ian how I'd had to put this woman to bed, and had taken off her knickers and everything - they were killing themselves.

The next morning when we saw Jim at breakfast he said 'Janette, I spoke to that old woman you helped last night and she was so grateful for what you did - but she's just wondering what happened to her jewellery'.

Ian: The only drawback about this trip was that there were 70 amateur magicians onboard having a convention - it was like being in the company of Paul Daniels, only 70 times worse. It was terrible. You couldn't walk anywhere without one of them trying to show you card tricks or pulling flowers from your ears. They were starting to really annoy us, but unlike Paul Daniels, there were so many of them I couldn't go around punching all their lights out.

Janette: This magician came up to me at the bar one night when I was in the middle of a conversation with Jack and demanded 'Pick a card'. I was like 'I'm actually talking to someone', but he was most insistent and said 'Pick a card, it won't take long'. So I did that and he then said 'Now sit on it'. So I did that too to keep him happy and he then said 'If I told you that you were sitting on the ace of spades what would you say?' I replied 'I'd say you know more than my gynaecologist'. He didn't like that reply so he skulked away, before returning about

15 minutes later with a dog he'd made out of balloons. He then started jiggling this balloon dog up and down between Jack Tinker and I at the bar. By this time Jack had had enough and took a pin out of his lapel and burst all the balloons. This magician looked at his hand, then looked at Jack and said 'How childish', before stomping off. But that's magicians for you, they can be right pains in the arse.

Ian: Magicians really are a bunch of weirdos, you have to be to spend six hours a day in a room by yourself practising tricks - but amateur magicians are even worse. I was chatting to Jim when another magician, came up to me with a huge handlebar moustache and speaking in a clipped manner like some sort of ex-RAF officer, said 'Caught the act last night, good start, then you lost them a bit in the middle, managed to get them back, then finished on a high'.

I looked up from my pint and just said 'Oh do piss off'. He looked mortified and said 'That's not very nice. I just thought I'd tell you what I thought'.

Janette: But we actually met some great passengers on board and our act seemed to go down well. The thing about the QE2 is that it isn't all snobby people like the two old dears from Edinburgh who'd been so mortified to see us on board. For many this is their first time onboard and perhaps they've saved up for years for a special anniversary, so the majority of them were great folk and we ended up having a smashing time.

Ian: The cabin was luxury personified too - unfortunately it spoiled us because after the QE2 we started working the cruise ship circuit for Airtours who'd regularly bung us in cabins down in steerage beside the huge turbines. There's nothing like the constant din of the engines to bring you back down to earth with a thump.

Janette: In 2001 we didn't do a panto that year after a few mix-ups with different theatres, but we'd never actually spent a Christmas or New Year at home and thought it'd be quite nice for a change. Then a tour operator called asking if we wanted to do the festive season in the Caribbean, and suddenly all notions of a romantic quiet time together in our home in Torquay flew out the window as we thought that sounded even better.

So we flew out on December 23 to Miami, but the flight was three hours late in leaving so we missed our connection to Jamaica. The next flight out wasn't for days, so we had to spend Christmas Eve and part of Christmas day in this hotel in Miami.

Our cruise ship booker then called and said we were to catch another flight on Christmas afternoon.

Ian: I thought the booker said we were going to Puerto Rico, which sounded great as we'd been there before and it's a smashing island with fantastic nightlife. However, a jobsworth immigration man wouldn't let us fly because we didn't have a return ticket. Even though I explained we didn't need a return as we were going to catch a boat, he wasn't having it and made us buy a return.

Then on the plane they announced the flying time, which I thought was pretty long for a little short hop down to Puerto Rico, but thought nothing more of it and we both fell asleep. Just as we were getting ready to arrive I was looking out of the window thinking 'This place is looking a bit scabby since the last time we were here' when the pilot announced it was 10 minutes before we landed in COSTA Rica.

Once we made it through immigration all the taxi drivers looked like drug barons. One of them took us to a hotel miles away, which was horrible. So instead of being on a huge luxury ship in the Caribbean for Christmas night, we were sitting in this cockroach infested little hotel. In the room which passed for a restaurant I asked for the menu and the waiter said there was no need for that as there wasn't much food. It was dreadful.

Janette: By this point I am thoroughly miserable and I've fallen out with Ian - as if it's all his fault - and was wishing that we'd stayed at home for Christmas, instead of starring in a remake of Planes, Trains and Automobiles.

Ian: But after a couple of bottles of wine we'd both mellowed and could almost begin to laugh at the situation. By this point it's now two in the morning and I said to Janette 'Come and get a good night's sleep and we'll feel better in the morning'. But the hotel owner heard this and said 'No good night's sleep - I have to drive you to the boat at 6am.' I was like 'Why do we have to leave so early?' And he simply shrugged and said 'Because it is a seven hours journey to the boat'. I thought 'This trip just gets better and better'. Sure enough we left at 6am in a beaten up old boneshaker of a car, feeling knackered and hungover for the seven hour journey over countless potholes to the boat. Any spirits we'd manage to raise the night before disappeared on that journey and Janette and I sat in silence.

Janette: We travelled right across the whole island that day, through rainforests and over ground that by no stretch of the imagination could be termed a road. It was awful. When we finally got to the boat and prised ourselves off of the sweat soaked seats, the first thing the ship's entertainment manager Lesley said to us was 'Where have you two been?' We didn't even have to reply as the murderous look on our faces said it all.

But then everywhere we went on the boat, all the punters were saying the same thing to us 'Where have you two been? We were looking forward to your show on Christmas day'.

Ian: Lesley then told us our cabin was taken as someone else had got in there first. I thumped my case down on the deck and said 'I'm going to be calm now Lesley, but if you don't get us our room I'm going to blow'. It was just one of those trips. When the timing has been thrown out of sync and it has this horrible knock on effect where everything else turns to crap.

I mean even the passengers were pains in the arse on this

journey. Normally on these huge ships the people are great and we would love to sit and chat with them for hours when we're not working. But what we discovered was that on these Christmas cruises, the ship is full of basically sad, miserable people who don't have friends or family back home, and that's why they go away.

So I'm standing on the deck by the rail looking out at the amazing feat of engineering as our huge vessel was being hoisted up 50ft through the Panama Canal, when this bloke from Manchester sidles up beside me, looks at this scene unfolding before our eyes and says 'Bloody hell, is this all it's about then? I might as well have stayed at home and looked at the Manchester Canal'. I just shook my head in disbelief. The whole ship was full of moaning miserable bastards like Mr Manchester Canal. It was dreadful and so unusual from the people we normally met on the ships.

Janette: The best part was when we turned up at the San Blas Islands of Panama, where the inhabitants, the Kuna, were all my height. I couldn't believe it - a land full of Jimmy Krankies. Not one of the adults could have been over 4ft 7in. The only difference was they had dead skinny legs covered in bangles, while I've got muscular legs from all my dancing. But they were all staring at me in as much amazement as I was staring at them. Then Ian gave me a nudge and said 'You better keep moving because they're stock taking.'

Shortly afterwards we docked in Kingston, Jamaica, then flew to Barbados to meet another cruise liner. But when we got to customs, another big officer asked us to open all our cases, when we were in a rush to make our flight. I thought to myself 'Oh no not again - I'm not missing another connection'. So I took out my Madonna wig and pointy bra and put them on - this female customs officer just burst out laughing and let us go through.

When we met up with the new cruise in Barbados we had

Hogmanay off so we went out for a meal on the pier with a magician from the ship Jamie Allan - one of the most normal magicians we've ever met - and his girlfriend Ayesha. It was a beautiful evening and so hot we decided to get our costumes after our meal and go for a swim. So when the clock struck midnight, the four of us were all in the water drinking champagne. It was idyllic and finally made the whole trip worth all the hassle.

33

FRENCH AND SAUNDERS

Ian: We weren't sent a script or anything, so we had no idea what French and Saunders were going to do to us. When we turned up at the studio Dawn French said 'I'm so pleased you came, I'm so pleased to meet you'. It was the first time ever that someone who was by far a much bigger star than we were, was gushing over us. It took us aback to tell the truth.

Janette: She said she used to love our shows and used to watch them all. It was a bit like meeting a fan.

Ian: We knew Dawn's husband Lenny Henry, because he had supported us during one of his first ever shows after he won New Faces in the early 1970s.

Janette: I asked how Lenny was getting on and she said 'Oh he never forgets his time with you playing in Glasgow'. I told her it was funny because I still had a poster with The Krankies top of the bill and Lenny at the very bottom - changed days eh?

Ian: But I couldn't believe the money which they had spent on this set, it was quality and we even filmed it in Shepperton Studios. Up until then I hadn't been a big fan of their show, although Janette always loved them. However, I still didn't have a clue what we were doing. I started to get suspicious when I bumped into Roy Hudd, Christopher Biggins and Bernard Clifton - I thought 'The old acts are all about to get sent up here'.

Janette: It was only then we were told it was a send-up of Silence Of The Lambs. We didn't think twice, we knew it'd be hilarious. Jennifer was playing special agent Clarice Starling, the role Jodie Foster portrayed in the film, and Dawn French was of course doing Anthony Hopkins' part of Hannibal Lecter.

Jennifer had to walk past all these dingy dungeon cells, with the different variety acts in them like us. So she walks past Roy Hudd and he sniffs the air and says 'I can smell...' and instead of saying that disgusting line from the movie which I'm sure you can all remember, he then adds '...insecurity, what you need is to get yourself an act and start treading the boards'. Jennifer then gingerly makes her way past Bernie Clifton's cell, who's standing there in his ostrich outfit saying 'What you need is to get yourself a gimmick - sophistication, that's the name of the game'.

Then she walks slowly past the last cell which is ours where Ian is sitting on the bed while I'm up at the bars dressed as Wee Jimmy, saying, 'Get yourself a catchphrase 'Fan-Dabi-Dozi! Fan-Dabi-Dozi!'

Dawn as Hannibal then says to Jennifer 'What did the Krankies say to you Clarice?'

She replies: 'Fan-Dabi-Dozi - it was horrible'.

Dawn adds: 'I'm sorry about that Clarice, it won't happen again'.

I thought it was simply brilliant. Ironically we were on a plane flying from Perth in Western Australia to Sydney when they showed that episode as part of the in-flight entertainment. All these South Africans were onboard and they were howling with laughter, then they realised we were on the flight too and they were all talking to us.

Ian: But Jennifer and Dawn seemed to like the Silence Of

The Lambs sketch so much they invited us back for another movie send-up, this time Batman and Robin alongside Patsy Kensit, who was doing Nicole Kidman's part while Janette was The Joker and I was Two Face.

Janette: The opening scene was at the gates of the asylum where they wanted my wee hand to come out from between the bars and lift the guard's hat while Ian thumped him with a truncheon and then Ian was to say 'Fan-Dabi-Dozi'.

Ian: But during rehearsals I improvised and said 'Fan-Dabi-Dozi - yer bastard.' They loved it and kept it in the sketch, although they bleeped it out - but you still see me mouthing 'yer bastard.' Then the prison chief says, 'Oh no - The Krankies have escaped - we need to call for Batman'.

Janette: Then we're supposed to have gatecrashed this posh dinner party, where I've to create mayhem, running around the table making a nuisance of myself, stealing people's jewellery. So every time the camera panned in on me I had another piece of jewellery dangling somewhere. Ian then says 'Whit's the matter with you?' And I say 'Uch, I'm just a woman at a bad age'.

Ian: We weren't told what to do, we just ad-libbed it all and they loved it and kept everything in. It was fantastic.

Janette: When I pass by Patsy Kensit, who Jennifer is trying to chat up, dressed as Batman, I start pulling childish faces and say, 'blah, blah, blah'. As soon as the cameras stopped Jennifer said 'I'm bringing in my video camera tomorrow to film you doing that - that's just the kind of thing my kids love'. So she did and got me to do that for her video camera.

Ian: I think they were amazed that we could do more than just Fan-Dabi-Dozi.

Janette: They were just lovely people, really down to earth. No angles to them, just straight down the middle. They treated it as a job and wanted to do it as best as they could. They were our sort of people.

Ian: Yeah, no airs or graces whatsoever - I've always found the people who put on airs and graces are the ones lacking in talent.

Janette: Then they got me back for a third time for a spoof of Stars Wars: The Phantom Menace. When Jennifer asked me I told her straight that I didn't have a clue about Star Wars as I'd never seen any of the films. So she sent me a copy of The Phantom Menace - a pirate copy as it was still out at the cinema at the time. I have no idea where they'd got it from, but it was a terrible copy and had obviously been filmed in a cinema with people coughing and eating popcorn in the background.

That was in 1999 and we were doing panto at the time in Glasgow so I went down to film it on my Monday off. When I got there the studio was roasting because of all the lights. Jennifer was playing Liam Neeson's part of Qui-Gon Jinn, who was to train me up as a Jedi, but Jimmy is creating mischief as usual. The first thing I say is 'If you're a Jedi how come you've got such big tits?' I then do the cheeky schoolboy ditty, pointing to all my private parts going 'Milk, milk, lemonade, round the corner chocolate's made,'

I also brought down a few props of my own, like a pair of Roy Orbinson glasses that spray water when I sing 'Crying' on stage. I showed Jennifer and she got me to use them too.

As usual with TV sets there was a lot of waiting about in-between takes. We were all in our costumes and it was so hot under the powerful studio lights, especially for Jennifer with all her leather on. It was a big production with tons of extras, but during the break Jennifer told me not to go with the other actors on the bus to get some food, instead I was to go back to their own personal trailer. So we had a little fan, one of those wee handheld ones, that we passed between the three of us to try and cool down. It came to five at night and we were due to finish at seven, but we were so knackered that the three of us lay down on the bed in their trailer. I'll never forget Jennifer lying on one side dressed as Liam Neeson with the beard, Dawn on the other dressed as Yodi or someone like that (I never did watch that pirate video so I don't really know who they were playing) and little old me lying in the middle dressed as Jimmy Krankie as usual, passing the fan between each other, and just talking nonsense.

I asked Jennifer if she had a boat in Salcombe and she explained that she and her husband Ade Edmondson have a boat on the Dart but they take it up to Salcombe. I said 'I knew that because last summer I was in Salcombe and I went into a fruit and veg shop only for the owner to say 'You're the second celebrity we've had in here this week, Jennifer Saunders was in too'. So we promised to look out for each other on the water.

I've got to say it was one of the most genuine and beautiful moments of my career. They really are fantastic girls and that memory of lying on the bed together will stay with me forever.

I'm just hoping they do Harry Potter soon and get me back for that too.

34

THE KRANKIES' KNOCKERS

Ian: We returned to Australia for a tour in 1985. That was our first visit to the continent since 1978. But because we'd been away so long one of the promoters reckoned that no one would remember us so they would need something to draw us in, so he came up with 'The Krankies Knickers 'N' Knockers Show' - complete with topless dancers.

I have no idea how it never made the papers because in 1985 we were well known as children's entertainers back home - and here we were on stage at the South Sydney Junior Leagues club with boobs flashing everywhere - the dancer's, not ours.

We later discovered the band The Bachelors were driving past and saw the billboard. One of them joked 'I can see the headline now - Kiddies' Favourites Cavort With Topless Models'. But we'd signed the contracts to appear, so thought 'To hell with it.'

The show was exactly as you'd expect in one of these huge Aussie clubs - very raunchy. Wee Jimmy was out on stage working with these big gorgeous topless girls. It was a good excuse for Janette to use all the old lines 'If you're drowning those puppies, I'll take the one with the pink nose' etc etc. The punters loved it, but then again they were all pissed and there were birds with their boobs out, so we really couldn't go wrong.

But before the show we were invited by the committee to join them in a banquet. Now the committees in these rugby league clubs are full of rather rough arse people, as you can imagine.

I got an instant taste of things to come as soon as I walked in the door of this astonishing grand banqueting room, and they all started shouting 'Oi mate, where's the fucking little fart?' referring to Janette, my wife. Normally that's enough to start my fists flying, but there were loads of them and they were all ex-rugby players so I wouldn't have lasted long. Instead I just groaned to myself 'This isn't a good sign at all, calling your headlining act 'The fucking little fart',' but as it turned out it was just a term of endearment and they all instantly took to Janette.

But their bawdy behaviour was in stark contrast to the food - which was literally fit for a king. I had never seen anything like it. Silver service, the biggest lobsters ever caught, prawns you wouldn't believe - surrounded by this bunch of barbarians, who were having food fights.

Just when I thought things couldn't get any worse, the chairman jumps up on the table, drops his pants and puts a 20 cent piece between his arse, hops the full length of this huge table, and drops the 20 cents into a pint tumbler. Another committee member then dropped his pants and lit one of his farts with a lighter. All at this black tie do. All in front of the guests and wives.

Janette and I were there with a French girl called Lisa Dore who'd come straight from performing at the Lido in Paris to Australia. She said to us 'Ieees do not believees this - these people are sooo crude.' I said 'Shhh - they're paying good money', but she was right. They were really rough.

But the thing is that's why I like Australia and the Aussies.

Here we were enjoying a meal that could be served at a royal palace, with folk being outrageous and wild - but really enjoying themselves. I think that's why I fit in down there, as I'm a wee bit eccentric like that myself.

Although sometimes that has backfired on me - even in Australia.

That same year we'd met up with the singer Tony Christie, he of the love songs, I did What I Did For Marie and, Is This The Way to Amarillo? We went to Manly on a day trip with Tony and we noticed all the workers coming off the boat from Sydney. They looked so miserable trudging off with their briefcases, shirts and ties. So Janette, Tony and I are sitting there having a couple of drinks when I say 'Look at all these miserable bastards, come on let's cheer them up - let's give them a song guys'. I decided to do one of Tony's numbers, got down on one knee amongst all these office girls and sang 'Give me your smile and the sunshine in your eyes', expecting Tony and Janette to join in. I turned around and the two buggers had done a bunk. They were hiding behind a wall, killing themselves laughing. So there I was, in the middle of this pier serenading these bemused and slightly startled girls.

35

BILLY CONNOLLY

Ian: We were working in Sydney in 1987, and took some time out one Sunday afternoon to stroll along Watsons Bay. Just as we were passing the famous fish shop Doyles someone shouted at the top of his voice 'Oi Krankie - I know your brother'. I'm thinking 'Who the hell is that?' And turn round to see Billy Connolly on the beach with his wife Pamela Stephenson and their two children.

Janette: I remember the kids were beautiful. Daisy was still in a pram at this point and they were completely covered with hats.

Ian: Surprisingly we'd never met Billy Connolly, but it is true that he really did know my brother Alistair. Billy had met Alistair years and years ago when he went over to Rothesay on the Isle of Bute in Scotland, where Alistair and his late wife Jean used to run the post office. He'd been asked over by Alistair to put on a show to help raise funds to save the local Winter Gardens Theatre, a project which my brother was hugely involved in.

Janette: It was funny our paths had never crossed until that point, but he was a great laugh and he shouted to his wife 'Oi

Pamela, c'mere and meet The Krankies', but I have to say Pamela wasn't in the least bit interested in the two of us. She sauntered over and meekly said 'Oh, Hello' and that was it. Billy then asked where we were working and I said 'At South Sydney Juniors Rugby Club', he was dead nice and said 'I've heard those big clubs are great'. Then I asked 'What about you?' And he simply replied 'The Opera House.' Talk about different leagues.

A few days later I was having a dress made in Sydney for the Water Rats Ball back in London and the gay guy who was the tailor was so proud of his creation he had me parading around this shopping mall in Sydney and of course who should be walking along with her babies in the pushchairs but Pamela Stephenson. I'm standing there with this evening frock on with a load of queens surrounding me, making a real spectacle of myself. Pamela was staring at me as if I was some kind of freak show, so I just shrugged my shoulders and said to her 'It's just a little number I'm having made for the Water Rats Ball'. She looked at me as if I was mad and snapped 'For what?' She didn't even wait for me to explain, she just gave me a little half smile and moved on. Now everyone in show business knows the Water Rats Ball. Remember Pamela may be Australian but she made her name on Not The Nine O'Clock News in London, so she would have been well aware of what the Water Rats were. Maybe I'm doing her a disservice and she may have just been painfully shy, I don't know. I don't know her at all as she only spoke four words to me despite me trying to be friendly to her. But what I do know was she simply wasn't interested in even talking to me. I didn't get any nice vibes off her on the two brief occasions we met. I'm just a gab who likes to talk to anyone, and I do mean anyone, no matter their status in life, as that's never interested me. But I did get the feeling that she looked down her nose at me.

But she should have known that at my height I've been used to that all my life!

That same year we also bumped into Max Bygraves at Sydney airport. We first met Max at the Royal Variety Performance in 1978. He was nice enough but always had a knack of making me feel uncomfortable by patronising me, as basically anytime he saw me he'd pat me on the head. We turned up at his home in Bournemouth once in 1986 and he was still patting me on the head. So when I met him in Sydney and he did the same thing again and I just blew my top. I don't know if I was still reeling from the incident with Pamela or that I'd grown much more confident since the first time we'd met, but I snapped back saying 'Would you stop patting me on the head every time you meet me - it's very condescending.' To my surprise Max apologised profusely then invited us to his house in Queensland in a place called, wait for it - Nobbys Creek. Only in Australia! It's miles from anywhere and he owned a huge chunk of land - as far as the eye can see.

It was so remote that a cow fell in his swimming pool and drowned once and it took three days for a forklift truck to get there and to take this bloated, stinking beast out of the water.

But he later moved from Nobbys Creek and bought an apartment just 500 yards from where ours was in Australia. We grew to be very fond of him and would always invite him for dinner. He would always reply, 'I don't do dinner, but I'll come for afternoon tea'. Whenever he was opening a club or casino he'd phone us up and we'd drive him there with his wife Blossom - who I absolutely adored too. So we became great pals after he stopped patting me on the head.

Ian: Anytime he turned up at a casino he would end up with half the place around him - he was a huge international star after all. But we used to have a secret signal, which means I have to make excuses like 'Right folks, we're up early tomorrow and have to go' Max would always mouth the words 'Thank you' afterwards. I loved hearing stories about how he first started out.

In fact Max told me once when he was young he used to play gigs in London in the early 1950s with Tommy Cooper. Max used to go on stage first then they'd walk to the next venue, with Tommy lugging all his props around with him. One night Max was on stage, waiting for ages for Tommy to turn up before he finally came flying through the door. Max was like 'What the hell happened to you?' Tommy then explained how he was so knackered trying to run from venue to venue he had to have a rest in the street outside a jewellers in Regent Street. A copper came along and asked what Tommy was doing there. He explained he was a magician, but the copper was having none of it so he made Tommy open one of his cases to prove it. This Bobby still wasn't convinced, so he then made Tommy perform a trick. The thought of big Tommy standing in Regent Street going 'Just like that' cracks me up.

But it's so interesting to hear how Max worked his way up from those wee clubs to become a huge star in America. He told me how he was at a function once with Jack Benny, Bob Hope and the woman who was with them, who got talking to Max saying 'Jack tells me you've just played the London Palladium and you're very funny - I must come and see your show'. Max said 'Thanks very much - and what do you do?' Well this woman just looked Max up and down then said 'Fuck right off', before turning and leaving. Jack Benny came over and said 'Hey Max - what have you done?' When Max told him what he'd said, Jack replied 'I'm not surprised she told you to fuck off - that's Joan Crawford'.

Another time Max took us to view a showhouse in a lovely suburb of the Gold Coast called Robina. The estate agent gave us the keys as he was showing another house somewhere else, so said we could view it ourselves. It was a blistering hot day, over 40c, and although it was a two million Aussie dollar home, the air condition wasn't connected yet. So we're all walking around sweating buckets when Max nips off to use the bog. He soon reappears and says 'I don't know what's up with the toilet, but it won't flush.' I said 'Oh don't worry, I'll take a look', thinking he'd just had a pee. But when I got upstairs he'd only gone and had a crap as the stench in this boiling hot house hit me like a shovel to the face. It turns out in Australia the aircon isn't the only thing that doesn't get connected until a house is sold - they don't turn the water on either. Needless to say we all left rather quickly and luckily the estate agent never had our mobile numbers to complain.

Janette: One of my favourite memories was when Ian's brother Alistair and his late wife Jean had come over to Australia. They loved having Max for tea and he seemed to have a great night too. In fact the next day he phoned to say how much he enjoyed himself, just watching Ian and his brother cook together.

Ian: Sadly Max died in 2012 at the age of 89 a year after Blossom. But he gave us some of the most sound - and blunt - advice we've ever received before he passed on.

After Janette's beanstalk accident we seriously thought about waving goodbye to the business once and for all. We were with Max one night in Australia when I told him our plans to quit and open a tearoom in Torquay.

Max replied 'Do you know how many scones you'd have to sell to make a grand? Don't be such a stupid prat.' And he was right. Shortly afterwards we were approached to do our first panto with John Barrowman at the Clyde Auditorium. Sometimes we all need that one person who will give it to you straight.

36

I'M A CELEBRITY...GET ME IN THERE

Janette: In May 2003 we ended up being invited up to Nobbys Creek again, but this time it was to the set of the ITV show I'm A Celebrity...Get Me Out Of Here.

Ian: We have an apartment in Tweed Heads and one day we were in a café by the beach and this Scots guy says 'I recognise you two.' It turned out he was a producer from the show. We got talking and he thought it'd be a great idea if we came down to the set and Wee Jimmy tried to break in. I thought it sounded fun, but we were in the country of holiday visas at the time and told him this. But he insisted that ITV would take care of it all.

Janette: A few nights later we then met the show's hosts Ant and Dec in the Tweed Heads Social Club. They're cracking boys but were absolutely knackered as they were working in reverse, staying up all night to do the show live for Britain.

Ian: Every Friday night Janette and I go to this club for a dance - the type of thing you just can't do at our age back home. But this particular night we were in with my cousin Robin who was over visiting us, when he spotted Ant and Dec and said let's go talk to them. To be honest I'd only ever seen them a couple of times on the telly and didn't really know what they looked like, especially across a dark crowded dance floor, so we waited until we saw Dec go into the toilet and followed him in - he must have wondered what we were all about. I said to him 'Excuse me are you...' and Dec shouted 'Wow - it's Ian Krankie, where's Janette?' That took me aback a bit, but he was a smashing lad and I told him that she was waiting for someone to dance with, as I've got two left feet. So we went back to the bar and he introduced Ant to us, who's Janette's favourite, and he asked Janette for a dance. She was made up.

Janette: It was brilliant because I was just standing there with Robin's partner Judy, when I got this tap on this tap on the shoulder, turned around and it was Ant McPartlin saying in that thick Geordie accent of his 'Hello bonnie lass - dae ye fancy a dance?' So we went up for a jig. He was a great laugh.

Ian: Ant and Dec must have been the youngest in the club, but they had a great time. They said they'd heard from their producer that we were in town and asked if we were going to come down and see them on set. I was actually dying to see the place as I'd heard it was incredible. A few days later we got to see it for ourselves and it was something else. There had to be something like 360 people working on it with scores of security staff - a security man even took a picture of our car's registration plate with a digital camera. It was tighter than the Royal protection squads. But for the sketch, I was to try and lift Jimmy over the fence saying 'This will get us back on the telly', before we're rumbled by a security guard, who chases us off - but not before Jimmy gives him a boot in the balls.

Janette: We were only in the jungle for an hour filming and I was eaten alive by bugs. I don't know what they were but they'd even managed to bite through my socks. I also ended up with a leech on my finger and I'd only just brushed past some bushes. I had literally been mauled just walking from the carpark to the set.

On top of all that, it was absolutely freezing and it was pouring down. The producer asked if I'd like to be considered as a participant for a future series, but I'd rather stay in my apartment. It honestly is miserable in the jungle and I wouldn't want to spend any more time in there than I have already.

Ian: We were then driving back to Tweed Heads the next day our journalist friend Matt called on my mobile, saying there had been a story in the English papers along the lines of 'The desperate Krankies try to get back in the limelight by breaking into the set of I'm A Celebrity.' As usual they had quoted an insider saying 'It was a pathetic attempt to recapture their fame'. I just laughed as it didn't surprise me. To think we'd taken a two day drive with Janette dressed as Wee Jimmy, to be eaten alive by bugs just to get back on the telly. No thanks. We honestly had no idea how bad the set was until we got there. We had just gone because we'd been invited by some really nice people. But there's no way we'd go through all that just for a TV show - those celebrities are welcome to the jungle.

Ian: Shortly after that we were asked to take part in a new I'm A Celebrity Get...Me Out Of Here-style show on ITV called Drop The Celebrity. I got a call from some idiot at LWT saying 'Am I talking to Ian Krankie? Oh cool it is you, cool, cool. I'd like you to take part in a new show called Drop The Celebrity. What happens is we take you up in a Hercules', then speaking to me as if I'm a child she added 'Have you ever been up in a Hercules? They're marvellous'. I deflated her a bit when I added 'Aye and bloody freezing. We were up in one with Lenny Henry for Comic Relief'. She continued 'Well there will be people in the audience who vote you off the show, then you'll be kicked out of the plane strapped to an expert in a parachute - it'll be great fun'.

I said 'Excuse me, let me stop you there. Did you know that we worked for LWT for three years and had our own show on primetime Saturday night and did three Christmas specials -

now you want to throw me out of a fucking plane', and slammed the phone down. I was furious. Kick us out a plane indeed - now there's an offer you can refuse. I'm glad I turned them down in such a marked manner, as Cheryl Baker from Buck's Fizz agreed to do the show and was the first to be thrown out of the plane and broke her ankle on landing. If that happens to us then we wouldn't have been able to work. And I bet the bastards make you sign a waiver before you jump too. We were never that desperate that we'd sit in some freezing cold, insect infested jungle or be thrown out of a plane just to get back on the box - no way.

Janette: I'm sure the public are getting tired of these shows too. It's voyeurism gone mad. They don't have any new ideas. The problem is they never nurtured great comedy writers in this country the same way they've done in America with Friends and Frazier and all the rest. The great talents who can write like Jennifer Saunders stick out like a sore thumb because they are so few and far between. So now we have minor celebrities being booted out of an aeroplane in the name of entertainment. It's sad.

Ian: You even had that Gillian McKeith show where the stars are given enemas, then would hold up a bottle to the cameras so you can see what's been taken out of them. That's the ultimate for me - actually showing shit on TV. Why bother developing a talent when all you literally have to show is a pile of shit.

Janette: Anyway we bought our Australian apartment in 2002 in Tweed Heads which is a beautiful place right on the border of New South Wales and Queensland beside the Tweed River - nothing like our Tweed river in Scotland as it runs out to golden beaches.

We would spend around three to four months a year there, going out straight after the panto season finishes so we miss the worst of the British winter and catch the end of the Australian summer. And when we weren't staying there we would rent it out. But after we'd spent our first summer in the new apartment a lady from Tasmania moved in, who was the perfect tenant as she wanted a long term let. She was also really cheery and would get up every morning to play golf and wore clothes which were young for her age, so we had no qualms about her moving in. Then just before Christmas that year we had a call from the Australian estate agent saying there had been a small problem with the apartment.

Ian: I'd taken the call and I told the estate agent to cut to the chase. I said 'What exactly has happened, has the tenant burnt doon the hoose?' But she said 'No, nothing like that, it's just, well, she's dead', and I said 'I'm very sorry to hear that, she seemed like a such nice woman' but the estate agent cut me off this time, adding 'Yeah, but that's not all - she died after she hung herself in your garage'.

Janette: We were left shocked after that call, but Ian broke the tension as usual, when he asked me 'Do you think she killed herself after finding one of our old videos?' I was then speaking to John Inman on the phone the next day and he was just as sympathetic saying 'Ooo Janette, what happened? Didn't she like your curtains? I feel like hanging myself too every time I see your drapes.'

37

MICHAEL BARRYMORE

Ian: We'd met Michael Barrymore on a couple of occasions over the years, the first was around 1986 in Max Bygraves' house in Bournemouth, when Michael was still with his missus Cheryl. But Michael is not a man you get to know. I reckon if we'd met Michael a hundred times we wouldn't have got to know him any better. He was a very strange guy and I got the impression that he never truly felt at home with the pros, maybe it was something to do with the gay secret he was hiding. I don't know what it was but he was always a very edgy character.

So imagine our surprise when we were on our four month sabbatical at our holiday home in Australia in 2003 and saw Barrymore advertised to play our local venue The Twin Towers Club.

It's a smashing club and always had great acts on. A few weeks before Barrymore we'd been to see The New Seekers and Petula Clark who really packed them in and put on fantastic shows. So when Barrymore turned up, we went along more out of curiosity than anything else because I couldn't imagine him packing in the crowds the same way The New Seekers had.

Sure enough when we turned up Barrymore was playing in front of a half full auditorium.

As a couple of pros sitting in the audience it quickly became apparent he hadn't done his homework - a few local gags always go down well, or a few jokes about the area's local neighbours, it's an old trick but it's something that will instantly endear you to a new audience.

Most of his gags seemed to be about his ex-wife. It was stuff like 'I was married twice - the first wife died, the second one just won't die'. After that one a woman in the audience started to cough and he said 'Don't you croak on me as well', but by this time the crowd were getting embarrassed.

I just got the impression that Barrymore needed his female dancers and an orchestra for his act like he had on TV. Instead it was just him on stage trying to interact with an audience that he didn't know and who didn't know him. He would do that thing he used to do at the start of his TV show, taking the piss out of the crowd. But that fell flat too. Instead he just rambled around on stage for two hours with no structure to his show whatsoever.

Now Billy Connolly is the master of looking like he has no structure to his shows, but believe me even a genius like Connolly knows exactly where he's going with his act. He may digress at certain points, but he'll know what he's starting and finishing with. Barrymore was just clueless.

He announced at the start of the show that he had the cold, and he probably did as it was turning into the Australian winter at the time, but that's no excuse. Announcing that at the start of the show is like giving yourself a get out of jail card. It's basically saying 'If I'm crap, then it's not my fault'. But he's supposed to be a professional. Pros work through colds, you have to or you don't get paid. Janette and I have never told an audience if we were feeling under par - they don't want to know or even care. They've paid their money for a night out, they couldn't give two hoots if you're stuffed up. Go and feel sorry for yourself after the show, but not in the middle of it.

To be fair at the end when he came off stage he got a decent round of applause - but the Aussies are always very accommodating like that. It was afterwards in the corridors outside the auditorium that I noticed the difference. It was completely silent. There was no buzz whatsoever, everything just felt flat.

Before the show we had the stage manager put a note under Barrymore's dressing room door, saying that we were in the audience, in row such and such. Now any pro in the world - especially ones that you've met before - will invite you in for drinks or a cuppa afterwards. But we heard nothing. He simply didn't want to know, which is unheard of.

Maybe he didn't remember us, maybe he didn't like us, but I suspect maybe he knew he'd been crap and just didn't want to face us - like I said he was never comfortable in the company of other pros.

A woman from the audience summed up everything when she said to me afterwards 'Isn't it sad to see him like that'. I think that's the worst thing someone could say. If people leaving our shows thought that of us like that we'd have stopped on the spot. But do you know, she was right. It was sad.

I read in the British papers at one point that Barrymore said he was going to immigrate Down Under, probably to New Zealand. That would probably have been a better idea because if I was him I'd give Australia a miss.

38

THE ENTERTAINERS

Ian: When we got the offer through to do the BBC show The Entertainers in 2002 I must admit I immediately sensed a stitch-up. But my agent assured me that the show would be playing it straight. What I didn't know was that Louis Theroux was one of the producers, or I would have probably said no. But just when you think the tide is turning against the world of political correctness, the BBC is still a bastion of PC. Our contact with the programme was with a director called Harriet and I swear the first words from her mouth were 'Hi, I'm Harriet and I'm a lesbian - does that bother you?' I said 'Why would that bother us? We've been in showbiz most of our lives.' She then explained that she is told she must tell people her sexual orientation before the interviews. I was completely baffled. I then had a question of my own. I said 'Why do the BBC want to present us as nice people? There must be some edge to this programme?' But she was insistent 'Oh no, you've been going for years and it's about time people saw you again', but frankly I wasn't convinced in the slightest.

The first bit of footage they wanted was me taking my Grand Banks motor cruiser out on the water. I took them on one of the most beautiful boat trips in Britain, from Torquay up the River Dart. But what I noticed was that Harriet and the camera crew weren't interested in any of the scenery whatsoever, and were concentrating on me - they were obviously wanting to catch me off guard. I spotted someone on the water I knew and had a quick chat. Afterwards Harriet said 'You seem more at ease with ordinary people than showbiz people - in fact you're not very showbizzy at all. Is Janette more showbizzy?' When she said that I knew I should have never agreed to filming. Then she asked 'Does it bother you that people don't recognise you anymore?' Again I was baffled. We've lived in Torquay for years. What was she expecting? The people we see and live with everyday suddenly ask for our autographs?

Janette: They never used any of that trip on the boat in the show because it was too beautiful. They wanted more of the tacky stuff.

Ian: For the next bit of filming they wanted to watch us doing a show, so they came down to Great Yarmouth, where we were playing the 1,000 seater British Holidays venue at the Seashore holiday camp - it was a fantastic place. Harriet had only been in our car for two minutes with her camera when she said 'Do you not think it's a big come down having to play these awful holiday camps?' I stamped on the brakes and pulled over. I said 'Now look here, not everyone goes to Tuscany for their holidays like you do at the BBC. This is what ordinary working people do on holiday and I'll tell you kids will have more fun here than they would on the Riviera.' Harriet then asked 'So will the dads all have tattoos and shaved heads?' But just before I was going to blow my top, Janette put her hand on mine and said 'She's just trying to wind you up for the show - don't rise to it.' So I drove on to the venue without saying another word.

We stopped at a café on the way there and were served by these two lovely girls from Birmingham. They were an absolute hoot and were kissing and cuddling Janette saying 'I can't believe we've met Wee Jimmy Krankie.' And I thought to myself 'I bet they don't stick that in the show because they want us to be a sad old pair of has-beens that no one recognises' and sure enough that part never featured either.

When we got there the organisers had laid on two £35,000 caravans for us and for the BBC and again Harriet just sneered 'Have they brought out the family silver just to impress us?' I took her by the arm and said 'Why are you being like this? All the caravans are like this here. People spend a fortune on them but you would never know that because you'd rather look down your noses at these folk without knowing what they're all about.'

During the rehearsals she then says 'Do you know, you've impressed me already - I didn't know you sang.' I just replied 'You don't know anything about us - we're more than just a wee boy in a school uniform.'

We did our show then told the audience the BBC were filming and of course the place went nuts. At the end there was a queue waiting for our autographs and Harriet said 'I can't believe it - they loved you.' That's when I knew they didn't want to show us in a good light. They thought we'd go on stage and bomb. I said 'Do you think if we were crap, we would have been around for 40 years? Not a chance.'

Funnily enough we ended up getting on well with Harriet. She was only doing her job - albeit trying to make us look like fools, but still it was her job. After following us for about weeks, she admitted she wasn't getting the kind of slant she wanted, so she asked if I'd get drunk and she'd film it, well I don't mind getting drunk on BBC money. So she filmed me getting pissed in our house in Torquay and I played it up for the cameras, jumping into bed and knowing that Harriet was a lesbian, I said 'Come on Harriet get yer kegs off and I'll show you a good time'. Of course they used that bit! Me acting up like an old perv. But she seemed to be pretty happy with that footage in the end, so I guess we helped her out.

Janette: Every time we're interviewed, the journalist or presenter are always after a slant like Harriet. There's not an interview that goes by where they don't ask about our 'curious relationship'. They believe there must be something seedy. We've had our moments as we explained in this book, but seedy? I certainly don't think so.

Ian: All we are is an Old Variety act, there's always been child impersonators in our business, but most people around these days won't remember that. They want to believe there's something off about us. They can't seem to understand that at the end of a show we go home and be ourselves, cook a meal and open a bottle of wine.

Janette: So the only footage they used of me in The Entertainers was going shopping in Sainsbury's and getting my legs waxed - gripping television! They focused more on Leo Sayer in the end because he really made a bit of an arse of himself.

Ian: I think they ruined the career Leo had only just recently managed to get back. The thing is I'm more than happy to take the piss out of myself for the likes of French and Saunders, because they're professionals. But this documentary lot are hopeless. Their show looked dreadful and was all done on shaky handheld cameras, it made me feel sick watching it - and the sound quality was dreadful too.

Janette: They didn't like it when we told them what we thought at the screening. They said it was meant to be like that, but I replied 'I can't believe anyone would deliberately make their show that shaky and practically inaudible.'

39

BANZAI

Janette: I was just about to leave Torquay for panto rehearsals at the Glasgow Pavilion for the 2002/2003 season when I got this request through from the Channel 4 Japanese betting show Banzai. It was fairly straightforward - they wanted Wee Jimmy to show off his boobs!

At first I thought 'Nah' then I discussed it with Ian and decided 'Well it's not as if we're Childrens' TV stars anymore'. Ian also reckoned it would help enhance our 'cult status' if we continued to do more on the university circuit as Banzai is a big hit with the students, but to be honest, I never thought that way and I did it because I'd always liked the show. I suppose a part of me was also just a little bit flattered at being offered in the first place, I mean Wee Jimmy has had to hide these boobs under a school blazer for decades and it was about time they had an airing. Jimmy may not have a willy - but he's got a nice pair of boobs.

But I doubt it raised many eyebrows because it's hardly shocking TV compared to what else is on the telly these days. It was actually really fun to do and completely different from what I'm used to. The producers had asked me to bring an assortment of underwear with me - the first time I've ever been asked to do that before going into a television studio. In the end they used me in a white bra and I have to say the final result was very funny.

A Banzai presenter says, in a heavy Japanese accent 'Today Banzai can

reveal a disturbing dark Krankie secret, because he is not really a Wee

Jimmy Krankie at all - he is actually a woman. But this is good news as it now means we can play A Little Boy Bra Size Bet. For the first time Wee Jimmy Krankie man/woman has agreed to reveal his boobs. The question is what bra size is he? Mr Krankie man/woman, will you please show us what you've got?'

I then pulled apart my blazer, to show off my bra and my only line was to then say 'They're a 34B - Fan-Dabi-Dozi.'

The Banzai presenter adds 'Wow - look at them, they're unbelievable. Brilliant stuff from the wee fella.'

Ian: At least now everyone can see why I've been hanging around with a cheeky wee schoolboy for all these years.

Janette: We actually got a really good response from that and The Sun even did a feature on my strip over two pages. Our friend Matt told me they had had great fun coming up with headlines that day. They originally had 'Krankies' Krackers' then 'See YOURS Jimmy' before finally settling for 'Fan-Booby-Dozi'.

It was all good fun and I enjoyed myself with the Banzai crew, who really looked after me, getting me first class rail tickets from Torquay to London and picking me up in a limo. When filming was finished one chap from the crew escorted me to my limo and as he closed the door he immediately got on his mobile, no doubt telling a friend 'I have just had the weirdest day with Jimmy Krankie'. As the limo pulled away I lifted up my blouse and gave him another jiggle. He just burst out laughing while everyone else around him looked at him as if he was daft.

But I doubt I'll ever be asked to strip off again as Wee Jimmy is getting on a bit, so I reckon he's missed his chance to do Playboy - or would that be Playgirl?

40

ABSOLUTELY FABULOUS

Janette: We were in the middle of our Australia break at the start of 2003 when we got a call from the Ab Fab office saying that Jennifer Saunders wanted me to play a part in the new series. The good news was the filming didn't start until we returned, so we didn't have to cut short our trip. I probably would have come back early if they'd asked because I was so excited about being offered an acting role.

When I got home to Torquay I called the producer and asked if they had a script yet as it was only two days to filming. The producer Jo Sergeant said 'Don't be silly - this is Jennifer we're talking about, she changes everything at the last minute', but Jo promised if she even had a rough draft she'd fax it to me before I left on the train to London. When the script came through there was hardly anything on it, except to say that I was playing a devil child. The story was that Jennifer's screen daughter Saffy, played by Julia Sawalha, was about to have a baby and Jennifer dreamt the child would be me dressed as the devil.

Then I was told I was also playing a Scottish midwife too. So I learned what few lines I'd been given and when I arrived in

London I did a read through at the studios with Jennifer and Ruby Wax, who also worked on the scripts for the show. I was unusually nervous as it's actually very daunting walking onto the set of such an established show and kept saying to Jennifer 'Please don't give me too many words as I'm only a turn - I'm not an actress'.

But when I came in the next morning for filming, the entire script had been changed again. What's more Jennifer had done just what I'd pleaded with her not to do and had given me even more lines. I was going 'Oh no Jennifer, what have you done to me', but she just said I'd be fine and told me to relax.

I had to film the devil baby part first. They had this little lovely blonde three year old girl playing one of Jennifer's dream sequences, then a little mixed race child for one of her other images, as Saffy is supposed to have met up with an African, so Jennifer doesn't know what colour the child will be.

The little blonde was wearing an all in one romper suit and goes up to Jennifer while she's in bed, then runs away and Jennifer gets up to follow her, but when she catches up with the girl she spins her around and it's me with a blonde wig in a romper suit going 'Haha - I'm a little baby and I'm coming to get you', before I pull out a huge knife and Jennifer faints.

Then the doorbell goes and it's me as a midwife and Jennifer gasps 'It's the devil child' and I go 'Oh scary, scary'. I'm shown to the kitchen and say to them 'Well I've got all the blah blah blah information that you wanted', before I spot their fridge full of champagne and add 'I could murder a drink', but they only get me a cup of tea.

For my next line I say 'Right I better get on with it', and take a pelvic bone and a baby doll out of my bag and start screaming 'Ahh ahhh, more drugs, more drugs', while squeezing the baby through the pelvic bone. I then tell Saffy 'I was in labour that long they had to shave me twice. Right I must be on my way, I've got an ante-natal class this afternoon, 30 waddling women squatting on the floor, focusing on their exit holes all imagining they can breath their way through childbirth. But I tell them, when push comes to shove, you'll be screaming for drugs and shitting the bed'.

But on my first take I fluffed that line and just looked at the studio audience and said 'Oh fuck it.' The place erupted in laughter. Afterwards I said to Jennifer 'I'm really sorry about that' but as usual she was so nice and said 'Don't worry about it, I always forget my lines and I write them - but Greg Dyke was in the audience and he loved it when you swore'.

I thought to myself 'That's just perfect Janette - my grand return to the BBC after all these years and I fluff my lines and swear in front of the Director General'.

But Jennifer was really full of praise. She said the most important thing was that my bottle didn't go and I was able to get the line done on the next take. I suppose that's the thing - I've always had bottle.

There is only one time in my entire career that my bottle went. I did this TV show for Channel 4 with Lulu, which was like a This Is Your Life, where they would spring surprises on the star guest. So for Lulu they would bring up things from her past, like first loves and relatives. Then they brought me in because Lulu had won a poetry competition at school and the gag was 'And here's the child that should have won it'. I was to walk out to meet Lulu and read her childhood poem.

But for the first time in my life I choked on my words. I completely froze. It had never happened to me before. But I reckon what had thrown me was that Lulu had so much botox in her face that the shock of suddenly confronting her under the harsh studio lights frightened me rigid. My bottle had completely gone and I couldn't carry on. Fortunately for me that show was cancelled and was never screened.

The thing is Ian and I had met Lulu years before around 1983 when we were in Eilat in Israel. She was in the same hotel with her then husband John Frieda and we'd meet for a drink at night. But I was honestly so shocked by how different she looked now that I couldn't go on. The whole experience upset me for a week. I started to think that maybe I wouldn't be able to go on stage ever again. But fortunately it never happened again.

I know a lot of people in showbiz go in for plastic surgery, but I've honestly never considered it. I mean I could probably do with it, especially since I was supposed to be playing a wee schoolboy, but really when I do Jimmy now it's a parody of Jimmy Krankie, because by no stretch of the imagination could I honestly pass myself off as a schoolboy now. That's why I was happy getting exciting roles like playing a fearsome old Scottish midwife on Ab Fab.

To me someone like Joanna Lumley gets even better looking with age and she's had nothing done. When I met her on set I thought she was simply stunning - a real classic looking woman. And what's more, she couldn't have been nicer to this wee woman from Scotland.

41

IAN'S FALL

Janette: We had just started a summer tour of New Haven caravan sites in June 2003 when I thought I'd lost Ian for good. We'd arrived at Butlins in Ayr and I don't know if it's just because we're getting older and slightly more cantankerous, but everywhere we go now there doesn't seem to be any professional light or sound men. It's all just kids.

So when we turned up in Ayr, the lights for the show were all in the wrong position and there was no one around who knew how to set them. Being a former sparky from the Pavilion Theatre, Ian gets a set of step ladders and asks one of the staff members to hold the bottom as he climbs up to adjust the lighting rig. Even though I was watching what he was doing I still don't know exactly what happened. What I remember was in a split second Ian seemed to take a little wobble and fell off the top rung of this 15ft high ladder.

It was horrible. Everything seemed to be in slow motion as he fell to the ground. He landed awkwardly with a huge thump. I immediately rushed over and told him not to move as I feared he'd broken his neck. He was in shock and ghostly white, but I made him lie there until an ambulance came. I think I was panicking more than Ian. The worst part was when the medics put an oxygen mask over his face, then put him on a stretcher and carted him into the back of the ambulance. I felt so helpless. You just see everything in your life being reduced to nothing. It's so easy to take each other for granted, but when you think you may lose your partner, the person who's always with you, panic really begins to set in.

We were in Ayr Hospital for hours having Ian checked out and fortunately he had just been left with a deep gash in his leg, but I think I was more shaken up than he was. We cancelled the shows for the rest of the week, but Ian insisted he got back on stage after just five days' rest - with stitches in his eight inch wound.

Since then Ian has been banned from going up any more ladders. I told him I don't care if the lights are in the wrong position - we'll perform in the dark if we have to.

But our shows still went down well in the caravan parks as we did a very fast one hour set. The longest thing in the act was Wee Jimmy which would last for about 20 minutes. Jimmy always got the biggest reaction. Parents would bring their kids in and say 'This is what your mummy and daddy used to watch'. If we didn't do Jimmy, there would be a riot.

Ian: We've always done well with working class people, they are our audience. We are working class entertainers and we've never been high brow. We come on with our dancers and perform hits from the charts and then would finish up with Austin Powers with me as Dr Evil and Janette as, who else, but Mini Me or whatever else was current at the time.

Janette: The camps were a good money maker for us, but hard work. It's like having a proper job, everyday we had to get up and hit the road, set up the gear, work till midnight then do it all over again. A friend of mine, who works in a bank, said

'But Janette, that's what most people have to do. They are routined - you've just been very privileged that you've only had to work for a couple hours a day most of your life'. I had never thought of it like that until she pointed it out to me.

42

A COUPLE OF CULTS

Janette: After popping up on various TV shows in 2002 and 2003, we got all these offers to play big bars like Brannigans in Manchester. Jade Goody from Big Brother had been at this venue the week before us and was supposed to do half an hour but only lasted 12 minutes.

And the week before that they had Spencer Smith from Big Brother and paid him £2,000 just to stand and chat to people at the bar. But they wanted us to do our act.

Well the place was packed to the rafters and the DJ forgot to put our mini disc on, so instead he just shouted 'Give it up for the Krankies.' Just then there was a fight in the corner and the place quickly turned into a riot. We surrendered after 40 minutes and couldn't wait to get out. It was just horrendous. The lights and sound were terrible and the crowd weren't interested - they were also all standing up so no one could see me. So we quietly left by the back door.

Ian: The next day the bar's owners at Hendersons phoned up asking us to do all the Brannigans bars across the country for £2,000 a gig. We couldn't believe it because it had been crap. But they didn't care as the venue had been packed out - that's all they cared about. But we turned them down flat. We're too old to be doing all that nonsense now.

Janette: In the same year we were asked to do our first university gig at Strathclyde University. There was a stand-up act who had been a big hit at the Edinburgh Festival who was supposed to do half an hour before us and he lasted just six minutes. All he did was eff and blind and the students simply didn't want that.

I have never been so nervous before a job in all my life. I was terrified, especially after this comic died on his arse. But that all disappeared as soon as we went on stage and there was this almighty cheer from everyone shouting 'Fan-Dabi-Dozi'. I then walked through the audience and instead of looking for 'me mam' I was looking for my sister. Ian asks 'What's she like?' and I say 'Bacardi Breezers' - the students loved it. This great big huge guy stood up in front of me and I said 'Hello big boy - do you know I'm the only person who could ever go up on you?' Well that was it, the place just erupted. It just shows, you don't have to swear. In fact we only swore once that night and that was only for the students. It was while we were doing the magic act and Ian tells me to get into the box and he'll pass a sword through my head and I shout 'Get tae fuck.' But that was it.

Ian: What was interesting was that all the audience were boys - there were only three girls in the crowd and we'd never realised until that moment that Jimmy Krankie must have been a boy's act. You can never tell when you do panto because the whole family is there and we only do Jimmy for a little while if at all.

I suppose it was like Dennis The Menace - Jimmy was a boy's hero.

43

THE ACCIDENT

On December 15th, 2004, Janette suffered a fractured skull and a broken collar bone when she fell from the top of the 20ft hydraulic beanstalk when it collapsed during a matinee panto performance of Jack and the Beanstalk at Glasgow's Pavilion Theatre. The bizarre, but nearly fatal accident, made headline news across the whole of the UK.

IAN: 'I don't like working with props and I don't trust this one.' That's what Janette told me right at the start of our panto run in 2004 at the Pavilion.

I assured her everything would be okay, but she had a bad feeling about it and I should have listened to her. Instead I said 'Let's go through with it.'

We were about half-way through a matinee performance when I heard this creaking noise, followed by a loud crack and by the time I turned round there was one almighty crash.

Janette was at the top of the beanstalk with the actor Gary Hollywood when it collapsed.

It's only when I saw her lying there, that you realise just

how small and fragile she really is. She was unconscious and bleeding from her ears. She looked like a broken doll. It was horrible, really, really horrible. There were children screaming everywhere.

Janette: I don't remember anything about the fall. But during the first few days of the run I badly strained a back muscle when I fell during a scene. It was the first time I've ever injured myself on stage and thought at the time 'Maybe that's a bad omen.'

But Gary and I had been complaining about the beanstalk from the start. It used to shake when it was at its highest point. We told the theatre's management but they accused us of mucking around and making it shake. But we weren't mucking about because we didn't feel safe on that beanstalk.

Ian: The next thing I knew, I was in the back of an ambulance with Janette being rushed to the Royal Infirmary.

The hospital was just a blur as they took Janette off for an MRI scan. The wait for the results was excruciating and I just kept thinking 'I can't lose her.' I wouldn't know what to do with her.

When the doctor came back with the results, I was told she had been lucky as there had been no bleeding on the brain. The bleeding from her ear had actually been a perforated eardrum from when her head hit the stage. But she was badly bruised and was black and blue all over. Her concussion seemed to clear overnight but she was so sore. I was also told it would be seven weeks before Janette would be well again. I had already decided we wouldn't be going back to finish the panto but that just confirmed it.

After just over a week in the Royal, I arranged for Janette to be transferred to a private hospital in the West End of Glasgow to continue her recovery. We stayed until Christmas Eve before we returned to our rented flat in Glasgow and had family and close friends over for Christmas Day.

People kept saying to us that this must be 'our worst Christmas'. But I didn't look at it that way at all because I could have so easily been attending a funeral.

Janette: We soon moved back to Torquay where the Pavilion sent the hundreds of get well cards they'd received at the theatre. It was really overwhelming and I burst out crying reading the messages. I also got a lovely card from Julie Walters and Jonathan Ross sent flowers. But Dawn French and Jennifer Saunders sent me fish. Seriously, one day a delivery driver turned up with a box with a warning label saying it contained live fish. Inside there were four beautiful snowy mountain minnows, with a note from Jennifer and Dawn saying 'We thought we'd send you some fish to cheer you up'. Only they would send fish instead of flowers but it definitely gave me a laugh.

Eddie Large from Little and Large, also wrote a funny letter offering to take Wee Jimmy's place in the panto while Bernard Manning said, 'So you've got to throw yourself off a beanstalk to get a laugh these days?'

But I was still very sore and very depressed. I couldn't believe that after all these years in showbiz I'd never experienced a bad accident, then a bloody beanstalk nearly killed me.

Ian: By the middle of February, Janette was fit enough to fly to Australia. I thought the change of scenery would lift her spirits. So we appeared on GMTV one morning to talk about the accident then flew down to Oz the next day.

Janette: We had only just arrived at our apartment when we were approached by Peter Kay who wanted us to appear in the video to his Comic Relief single where he mimes (Is This The Way To) Amarillo by our old friend Tony Christie. But at this point we had just started our three-month stay and I was in no fit state to make the journey back to the UK so soon. It's a real pity because Ian and I are huge fans and would love to have worked with him. We eventually got our chance, but more about that later. But right at that moment and time the Australian sunshine was doing us the world of good.

Ian: We got our chance though when Peter came back in for us three years later for another Comic Relief single I'm Gonna Be (500 Miles) by The Proclaimers which also went to No1. So finally we had a hit record.

Janette: But while I was recovering in Australia, Dawn and Jennifer got in touch to see if I'd be interested in making their Christmas TV special. This would be the sixth time I've worked with them, as I've done four French and Saunders, one Absolutely Fabulous and a Murder Most Horrid with Dawn too. I said yes, but inwardly I was apprehensive as I hadn't worked since the accident and still didn't know if I could.

We flew home at the end of May and I arrived for filming at Pinewood Studios in July where the first thing Dawn asked me was 'How's the fish?' I had to confess I'd given them away as I'm no good with pets. She then asked me how I was with pirouettes, as they wanted me to do a spoof of Billy Elliot.

They also had me doing other sketches including Dustin Hoffman's role in The Graduate, to Billy Flynn from Chicago and then Dawn asked me if I'd be okay with lap-dancing? I told her as long as I didn't have to climb up the pole I'd be all right, as I haven't had much luck with heights lately.

But I performed the lap-dancing scene in front of a live studio audience, and hearing them scream with laughter as I was writhing around this pole really helped get my confidence back. Afterwards Dawn said to me I'd got the biggest laugh of the night. It felt good to be back.

Ian: Janette had lost her confidence but Dawn and Jennifer really helped her get it back. But she was still suffering from side-effects from the fall. We'd been to see an ear specialist about her hearing because of the perforated her eardrum and then needed to have a molar removed, because it had cracked in two on impact. We then got a chance to perform on stage at our old stomping ground, Blackpool's North Pier for the summer, where we still hold the record for 142 consecutive sell-outs.

On the bill were our mates Bucks Fizz who also helped Janette a lot. For the opening show Janette came down the centre aisle in a wheelchair with a stookie on and the palace erupted. After that we knew she would be fine.

Janette: But when I was packing for Blackpool I found a hospital bag with the Jimmy Trott costume I had been wearing on the night of the accident.

It had been sliced in half by the medical staff as they had cut it from my body. When I saw my own blood splattered over my white collar I burst out crying.

I still had no memories whatsoever of the fall, but seeing the costume made me realise just how serious it was.

44

NEW BEGINNINGS

Janette: It felt strange coming up to Christmas 2005 with nothing to rehearse for. With nothing better to do we decided to make the most of the time off and head for London for a break and a bit of Christmas shopping and try and figure out what we do next.

Ian: Our friend Tommy Gorman was going to London to see his daughter and invited us to come and meet him in a cafe in Kings Street, Covent Gardens. I was sitting there when I said 'I think the Qdos office is around here.'

Qdos was owned by Nick Thomas who used to do a puppet act back in the early 80s, but was also working as a promoter too. He asked us to sign for him but at the time we still had a two year deal to run with Lord Delfont.

The next thing I heard was Nick was doing a show called Rock with Laughter at the Grand Theatre in Blackpool with Keith Harris and Orville. Getting into the Grand Theatre made many sit up and take notice of him in the business as it was a prestige venue and Nick was doing good business there. He approached us again to do a pantomime but we were still working with Apollo Leisure who were at the time the No1 panto company in the UK.

Things changed when Lord Delfont decided he was retiring, so Nick came back for a third time and asked us to do a summer tour with him. It would start on a Sunday at the Grand Theatre, then on the Monday we'd be in Llandudno, Great Yarmouth on a Wednesday, Lowestoft on a Thursday and back to the Grand for Sunday.

It was a 15 week summer season in a tour bus with Great Soprendo again along with a singer and dancers. It made a lot of money for him and for us too. In 1985 we then did our first panto for him in Paignton in Devon.

The next year we were due to do Weymouth but when we went back home to Guernsey for a break we were watching the local news BBC South West, who reported that Torbay Council had lost quarter of million pounds that year from their leisure budget, when 'The Krankies had topped the bill' in panto. I nearly fell off my chair. The leisure budget also covered libraries, museums and public parks but we were getting blamed for the council's mismanagement.

Two days later Weymouth cancelled on us fearing that The Krankies would sink them too. That's how fickle this business can be - one misleading report can scupper you.

But Nick managed to get us another panto at Newcastle's Theatre Royal with Bernard Breslaw from the Carry On films and Anita Dobson from EastEnders and it did colossal business.

We worked with Nick right up until he sent us to Bournemouth, which I didn't really fancy as it's more of a summer resort but virtually dead in the winter. We were on the bill with Buster Merryfield from Only Fools and Horses, and the javelin throwing athlete Tessa Sanderson in Robinson Crusoe. Tessa was playing Girl Friday and had to wear a skimpy brown outfit but would always ask me 'Does my bum look big in this?' I always said no, until the show where she was wearing white knickers instead of brown. I said 'Tessa, know how you're always asking me if your bum looks big, well it looks fucking huge today as you're wearing white knickers.' Tessa went 'Oh no - I forgot to change them.'

Anyway Nick then joined forces with a big showbiz agent Paul Elliott and I knew we were definitely not Paul's type of act. Not long after I got a letter from the company saying 'It has come to our attention that you are using lewd and vulgar material.' I phoned them up straight away and gave them some lewd and vulgar material all right. It turns out they said my dame was too camp, which is ridiculous as that's what a dame is. As far as I was concerned we were finished, so I called the Glasgow Pavilion and told them we wanted to come home, which we did from the mid-90s until the accident.

Now here we were again without a panto to do when on a whim I decided to see if I could find Nick's Qdos office, which turned out to be two doors along from the cafe. I opened the door and who should be standing there but Nick himself. It was the day of their Christmas staff party which was starting at 1pm. He asked if Janette was with me then said come back for the party as the surprise guests.

We got a tremendous reception with everyone clapping when we arrived and then making a big fuss over Janette asking her how she'd been since the accident.

Janette: Nick then turned to his business partner John Conway and asked 'Who do we have for Darlington next year?' John said he had only booked Denise Welch so far for the fairy Godmother, then added 'Janette can play Buttons and Ian can be the Baron'.

Ian: No money was mentioned at this point, but it didn't matter as we were back with the number one pantomime company in the UK and Darlington was one of our favourite venues where we first played during the panto season of

1978/79. Back then we did so well there they had to add two extra weeks on to the end of the run and we returned there for the next two seasons.

Qdos came up during the last week for the end of show party, and asked if we fancied Wolverhampton next year. Once again we had been there before, doing pantos along with our variety shows, plus The Good Old Days BBC programme, so we knew it well.

It did great business yet again and we stayed for three seasons, but at the end of the third the owners of a rival company called First Family Pantomimes wanted to meet us after the matinee. So sure enough, when we came off stage they were shown to our dressing room and offered us a panto back in Glasgow at The King's Theatre. They said if we didn't fancy that we could choose one of their other venues. They seemed really keen to have us but I told them we would think about it, as it's not just a matter of saying 'yes' on the spot as you have to check the production quality, the characters they want you to play and your billing too.

But just as they were leaving our dressing room Nick Thomas and Michael Harrison from Qdos arrived, so the two biggest pantomime companies in the land came face to face at our dressing room door. Well, if looks could kill...

Nick asked his rivals what they were doing here and they said they had just come up to congratulate us on our performance.

That night we went to a Chinese restaurant with all the cast when Michael said 'I know they came to poach you - what did you tell them?' I was honest and said 'I told them we had nothing fixed yet for the following year'.

Michael glanced at Nick and then back to us and said 'Keep this to yourselves, but we intend on hiring a large venue in Glasgow to launch a pantomime with John Barrowman and we want you to headline it with him. It will be Aladdin and it will be spectacular.'

The name John Barrowman didn't ring any bells right away then I remembered seeing him in the West End years ago in Matador during the late 80s. We had also started watching the Doctor Who spin-off Torchwood on a recommendation, and realised it was the same guy from all those years ago.

'John Barrowman' I said, 'That could work.'

Janette: But when we met John for the first time at rehearsals we had second thoughts. He was very cagey with us at first and said 'They tell me you're the best in the business and will teach me all about pantomime.' I think his nose was out of joint because John had been doing panto for years.

Ian: John may have been cagey at first but our humour clicked and I mean socially, while he also clicked with us on stage too. He quickly realised that he could join in the laughs with us. Some pros are very protective of their act, usually the rubbish ones, but we've always been welcoming to others.

Janette: Although John always had the annoying habit of picking me up and twirling me upside down every time he saw me, even if I was walking down Buchanan Street doing my Christmas shopping, where, all of a sudden, I'd be getting thrown about in the air like a toy.

Ian: We started off at the SEC in Glasgow in 2010 with Aladdin and ended up doing more pantos with John than anyone else during our careers. The next year we did Robinson Crusoe and then Jack and the Beanstalk, Dick McWhittington and Cinderella

Janette: Jack and the Beanstalk was in 2012 which was eight years after my accident. Believe it or not I was keen to go back up the beanstalk again as it was a way of putting the accident behind me once and for all.

I'd had nightmares about the fall for a year afterwards but it's always best to tackle your demons head on and this was the perfect way to do it. I also trusted Qdos. They and their technical teams were amazing. We had total faith in them.

Ian: But there was an incident in the show…

Janette: It wasn't with me though it was with John this time. It was just after New Year when the horse we used in the panto got spooked and threw John off like a bucking bronco.

Ian: The horse was scared as a piece of scenery collapsed behind it on the way to the stage and it just freaked out. John was riding bareback so when it reared up it threw him off and he landed right on top of his coccyx. Anyone who's ever done that will know exactly how sore it is. So the fact John was able to finish the scene shows just how brave he was about it.

Janette: John was in a lot of pain backstage so came out and told the audience that he needed to go and get himself checked out. When the ambulance came and gave him oxygen I was holding his hand greetin'. I thought to myself 'What is it about this bloody show - it must be cursed.' Fortunately there were no broken bones and John was able to finish the run.

Ian: Although when I asked Nick Thomas if he was insured for a horse riding accident he said 'Of course' but went awfully quiet when I added 'Bareback?' Anyway John took a season off in 2015 so we ended up doing Peter Pan with David Hasselhoff. David was a nice man but his knees were knackered and he had zero energy or even movement on stage. The sword fight scenes were comical for all the wrong reasons as David remained rooted to the spot.

Janette: Working with The Hoff at least gave me a chance to do my Pamela Anderson routine with inflatable boobs of course. But after five years at the SEC I had itchy feet and wanted a change. I've always been like that and never like to stay one place too long.

Ian: In 2016 we teamed up with John again for Dick Whittington at the Birmingham Hippodrome for what was probably our best ever pantomime. The venue was just amazing, with a new building, dressing rooms and a staff canteen, built around an old theatre. In Birmingham the kids come to the matinee shows but the night time ones are almost exclusively an adult affair. We loved those shows.

Janette: We have such fond memories of those times with John. Ian would always make him some soup and we'd have that before the shows. We've even been out to LA twice to visit John and his husband Scott.

Ian: The last time I had messaged him to say we were flying from Australia and planned to stay at a hotel in Los Angeles, John messaged straight back and said 'You will do nothing of the sort - you're family' and he certainly made us feel that way. Of course 'they' have since tried to cancel poor John after an old Doctor Who video clip of him at a Comic Con went viral where the actor Noel Clarke threw him under a bus but claiming John was always getting his willy out on set. That was foolish, but we've all done foolish things in the past and there had been no complaints about his behaviour, but all of a sudden John was persona non grata at ITV and soon afterwards dropped as a judge on Dancing on Ice. To his great credit John has refused to give up or give in, but Janette and I would also soon experience what it's like when people try to have you cancelled...

45

DEATH CURSE & BEING CANCELLED

Janette: In 2016 we lost a lot of pros we knew well. We had fallen out with the magician Paul Daniels, partly because of what we wrote about him in this book, but had made up with him when we did a summer tour of the UK. Paul and his wife Debbie McGee even came to visit us in Australia in 2015. But by March, 2016, he was dead from a brain tumour at the age of 77. Thinking back to his time in Australia, it may have been the start of his illness. He wasn't very keen to go sight-seeing. Debbie would come to the beach with us a lot to swim, but Paul just wanted to sit in our place playing on his computer.

But he did love it when we took him up to see the area where I'm A Celebrity...Get Me Out Of Here is filmed. It's in a beautiful valley with all these waterfalls. That was the only time he really joined in.

In the same year we also lost Ronnie Corbett, from Motor Neurone Disease at the age of 85 and Victoria Wood. While David Bowie, Terry Wogan and Carrie Fisher had all passed away too.

Perhaps because we were both about to turn 70, Christopher Biggins was one of the first to call us to ask, 'Are you two feeling alright?'.

Then every time another one died we got more and more phone calls from family and friends asking if we were okay. It was as if people expected us to be next.

Ian: We first met Ronnie Corbett in the 1970s when we performed together on Guernsey and we had sailed over on our own boat. He couldn't believe that we had managed to find the island. He said 'How do two comedians know how to navigate a boat?'

Janette: Probably the biggest shock though was the death of Victoria Wood from cancer at the age of just 62. That one hit us hard, especially because she was a lot younger than us.

I'd had a little bit of a health scare myself that year after I had gone to see a specialist on Harley Street because I was having problems with my back. It was nerve-wracking as you fear the worst. But he told me it was osteoporosis and I had a 15 per cent chance of bone breakage and 35 percent chance of breaking a hip in the next 10 years. So he now gives me an injection twice a year to help slow down the problem.

Ian: Janette's back hadn't been right since the Beanstalk accident. The specialist told us it could have been from the shock to the body from the fall. But we still had no plans to give up panto and the following season we were sent to do Dick Whittington with John Barrowman in Manchester this time.

However just before Christmas 2017 a mum called Natalie Wood from Bolton publicly called for our show to be cancelled.

Our crime? She was appalled by the panto's double entendres - had she never been to a panto before? She also objected to the line 'Alice loves Dick' and Jimmy Krankie poking his finger out his fly like a wee willy as he has done for the last 40-plus years.

Her demands made almost every newspaper and were discussed at length on BBC Breakfast, GMTV and countless radio shows. But calling for things to be banned is a form of fascism. How can one person insist that the 1,800 people who had been falling about laughing at us every night, shouldn't be allowed to watch us at all?

Janette: I thought that young mother was a total pain in the arse. If she hadn't liked the show that much, why hadn't she just asked for her money back?

But what I didn't understand, and still don't, is how can just one complaint from one woman run for so long across all the media?

Ian: I first knew something was up when I woke to a message that we were on the BBC Breakfast News. All I could think of was 'What have we done now?' The local evening paper had also splashed on the same woman calling for our show to be closed. And it was still being discussed on BBC Five Live a week later. It's only a panto for goodness sake.

Janette: In all my career I have never had anyone calling for me to be banned. I made a willy joke on The Royal Variety Show in front of the Queen Mum who laughed.

Ian: Today's snowflake generation wants to be outraged. I think mainstream comedy is getting harder to do in this country when you now have people coming to your shows waiting to be offended so they can take to Twitter and Facebook and moan about you.

But the audiences were absolutely fantastic in Manchester where you would get real belly laughs, just like Birmingham and Glasgow. But of course it only takes one person to try and destroy all of that.

Janette: We had great support though. Biggins went on breakfast telly to defend us, saying there was nothing sleazy about our act, while TripAdvisor even gave us five stars reviews with people saying it's the best panto they've ever seen. But no one listens to them - just the one woman who made a lot of noise. And I still did the willy gag gag every night in

Manchester where the audience gave me an extra loud applause.

Ian: It was so ironic as we started the year being voted The UK's Best Panto Double Act and by the end of it we're having to defend our very existence. Sometimes you feel that the world truly has gone mad.

46

TAINTED MOVIE ROLE

Janette: In December 2015 we arrived in Glasgow to launch the Peter Pan panto with David Hasselhoff when I had just been offered a part in Absolutely Fabulous: The Movie. It was to be my first ever film role and I was to play the Japanese fashion designer Huki Wuki alongside Joanna Lumley and Jennifer Saunders as Patsy Stone and Edina Monsoon. I was really excited about it as I having appeared in the Absolutely Fabulous TV series as a devil midwife. But as usual I told our biographer Matt about the film role, who promptly printed it in The Sun. The very next day Ian took a phone call from one of the film's producers shouting the odds that I had ruined the movie's big surprise and they were now considering ditching the part altogether. If they were expecting a humble apology then they obviously don't know me, as I told them they could stick their film up their arse.

Ian: No one had told us we weren't allowed to say anything and now they were threatening Janette that she would lose the part. Of course after Janette told them where to go they changed their tone when they called back later. I suspect this was after realising that they may lose Janette altogether. But worse was to come for the producers when Huki Wuki became part of an international race row after the US-based Korean actress Margaret Cho branded Janette a 'yellow face' - apparently that's a white person who portrays an Asian person. She took to Twitter to rage (do people do anything else on Twitter?) 'Hire Asian actors for Asian roles. Yellow face is racism. I am fucking sick of yellow face.' She sounds nice!

Janette: We started getting calls from the press and again all I could think of was 'What have I done now?' It's definitely the first time I've been accused of being racist and The Krankies played the Chinese policemen in Aladdin numerous times over the years.

Of course Margaret Cho was missing the point. As always, the joke was about my height and nothing to do with the race of the character. It's also a comedy film, with a role for a very small comedy actress - who else were they going to cast?

When I was sent through pages and pages of the script with my scene, I realised I didn't have a single line to say. That was fine as it meant there was less stress on me when it came to filming. Although I did think it was funny that I'd waited all these years for a film part and didn't get to say so much as Fan-Dabi-Dozi.

But after the whole racism row kicked off, the filmmakers decided to have me talking as myself, to show I'm not really Asian. So when Alex Jones interviews me on the red carpet in the movie, I reply 'I need a piss' so people are left in no doubt it's definitely Janette Krankie up there on the big screen.

I loved filming though and on the days I was on set there was Jerry Hall, Emma Bunton, Lulu, Kathy Burke, Kate Moss, Richard Arnold and Amy Childs. It was funny though as I wasn't really given much direction for the scenes. All I had to do was walk about the room where everyone is supposed to be in awe of me.

I also got to work with Gwendoline Christie who at 6ft 3in is the tallest woman I've ever met - I only came up to her waist. She took pictures of us together on set and showed them home to her boyfriend, who thought they were hysterical. She then sent them to all her friends.

And Jennifer and Joanna were so nice when they saw me again. They made a real fuss. They were all lovely to me and it was great to meet Lulu again (this time I wasn't so shocked to see her) and also Kate Moss for the first time too.

Me and Ian were also invited to the premiere in July of 2016 in London so we got to hit the red carpet.

Ian: It's just a pity the movie was shite. I suggested a couple of lines on set that would have made some of the scenes funnier, but they weren't interested.

Janette: I don't think the race row helped much. It meant the film was slated before anyone had a chance to see it.

Ian: Margaret Cho later admitted the racism stuff was a load of rubbish. Matt interviewed her for The Sun and she revealed her accusations actually backfired on her. She said 'I had no idea The Krankies were so famous. I'm an American so I just didn't know. Then I'm talking about a British institution that the Brits are very loyal about. Suddenly I had this huge backlash with people saying to me, "Don't you understand The Krankies are of huge cultural significance - this means nothing to you because you're American". So I took that on board. I get it now. Totally. The joke was on Janette's height. Not being Asian. It just didn't translate for me because I'm always campaigning about race, so it was an education when people were saying, "The Krankies are beyond race".'

I'm not sure about the 'cultural significance' stuff but I suppose that's an apology of some sorts.

47

ANT AND DEC

Janette: In 2017 we had a chance to work with Ant and Dec.

Ian: Yes, unpaid work. It was shortly after they'd both signed a £30million three-year-deal with ITV, so maybe there was no money for anyone else.

Janette: Their production tried to get us for a skit for Saturday Night Takeaway. They wanted us to dress as Ant and Dec alongside Phillip Schofield and Holly Willoughby. Then Ant and Dec would judge who does the best impression of them. But it was to broadcast in February so it was of no benefit to promote the panto in Manchester.

Ian: We were being asked to travel from our home in Torquay for three hours to London, four hours filming in character and then back again the same day - all for nothing. I said 'We've been too long in this game to start working for free'. So I asked them for Equity Union rates.

They came back saying they couldn't afford that much, but could give us £100 each. I told them that was an insult and ended the call. I know that derisory offer wouldn't have been anything to do with Ant and Dec, but come on, the production company wouldn't even stretch to a hotel for the night.

Janette: That wasn't the only show we said no to. The previous year I was approached by the Channel 4 soap Hollyoaks to play a recurring character. They emailed an offer through but it just didn't suit me as it's filmed in Liverpool and you are on call for three months over the summer, which meant we couldn't nip over to Spain or see our friends. We have worked all our lives, so it's nice to be able to finally say no to things.

Ian: I'm glad we did as it turned out the role was as some evil Scottish granny who steals a baby.

Janette: That would have ruined my panto career on the spot. Jimmy has never been the baddie. I've never watched Hollyoaks, but people told me the character was really evil and twisted. It's a bit late in the day for me to start playing a villain.

Ian: When the story came out in the press Hollyoaks then denied they had ever offered Janette the role. But I have it in black and white on email. Why issue a daft statement like that? Is no one allowed to turn down Hollyoaks? It's hardly like saying no to Ridley Scott or Martin Scorcese is it?

Janette: I was also offered a part in the play The Wedding Singer, this time playing a rapping granny. I quite fancied that. And I'll also have to accept that at this stage of my career I'm only going to be offered granny roles.

Ian: We were also offered £500 between us from Who's Doing The Dishes on the BBC. They wanted to come and film us in our home for the entire week. But we didn't want cameras in our house for a whole week so they said they could rent us a place if we wanted instead.

I thought the whole point of the show was it was supposed to be in the person's home. But there you go, they would happily spend more on a rental than they were paying us to do it.

Janette: But I did say yes to David Walliams when he asked me to appear as Nicola Sturgeon on his BBC sketch show Walliams & Friends in 2016. I like David a lot and think he's very, very talented. When we got to the studios the first thing he wanted was his picture taken with us and his mum Kathleen.

I played Nicola opposite David who was appearing as David Cameron on Question Time where we end up in a heated argument about Harry Styles new haircut.

I say 'We in Scotland feel there are much more pressing issues facing us today than Harry Styles hair. Let him have it however he wants – as long as it's dyed ginger.' Sadly the sketch was dropped from the show which is a shame because Nicola is always being compared to me.

We were listening to LBC radio one day when an angry Scotsman came on the phone-in and said 'It's time Wee Jimmy Krankie behaved himself.' I was lying in my bed thinking, not for the first time, 'What have I done this time?' Until I realised he meant Nicola Sturgeon.

Ian: Read the comments on Mail Online under any story to do with Sturgeon and it's full of Jimmy Krankie mentions - all of them derogatory.

But I actually think it's unfair...on Wee Jimmy! Richard Littlejohn explained in the Daily Mail when Nicola resigned as First Minister in 2023, that he had always referred to her as Wee Burney after the son of alcoholic waster and self-styled 'creme de la scum' Rab C. Nesbitt in the BBC Scotland comedy. Richard wrote 'The reason I chose that moniker was because Rab C's Wee Burney was a malevolent character, a poison dwarf. Jimmy Krankie was a much-loved figure of fun. And, to my mind, there was nothing amusing about Sturgeon. Malevolence is her middle name.'

I agree. Jimmy was cheeky but never mean.

Janette: But then Jimmy's connection with Nicola was all over the news again in 2020 thanks to Boris Johnson!

Ian: We ended up on the front page of the English Sun after Boris got into a row with some woman who was organising COP26 (Claire Perry O'Neill) who apparently suggested Boris should offer Sturgeon a formal role to stop The SNP from trying to own the climate summit that was to take place in Glasgow the next year.

Boris allegedly replied 'Over my fucking dead body. I'm not being driven out of Scotland by that bloody Wee Jimmy Krankie woman.'

Janette: We were at our home in Australia again and yet again when we were contacted by the press. I can't get any peace anywhere.

Author's note Matt: When I was asked to speak to Ian and Janette for a comment on the Boris story, I called them in Australia at about 1am local time. They didn't answer. I told my editor that I feared I'd missed them as they must have gone to bed as it was the early hours of Wednesday morning. But fear not, Ian called me back about half an hour later when he and Janette had rolled in from their local club. These two have better social lives than the Gallagher brothers!

Ian: We obviously got to know his dad Stanley while doing The Real Marigold Hotel in 2017. So I gave the comment 'If Boris meant it as an insult to Jimmy, we'll be having words with his dad.'

Janette: I might not agree with Nicola's politics, but I've always admired her as a person. The closest we came to meeting was when we waved to each other from two passing taxis.

Poor Nicola has been compared to Wee Jimmy for years and probably always will be. I find it funny, although I wasn't sure she would like the comparison until Matt once asked if she ever got annoyed by it. It turned out she grew up with us like he did, as they were both born in 1970. Nicola told him 'I actually like

Jimmy Krankie. I think most people just use it as a bit of fun, but some on social media get really nasty with it.'

And that, dear readers, is why I am not, and never will be, on social media.

48

THE REAL MARIGOLD HOTEL

Ian: Out of all the shit TV shows we have been offered, for none or next to no money, finally our ship came in with The Real Marigold Hotel.

Janette: Ian and I loved the show and I always said that would be the only thing I'd be interested in doing, spending a whole month in India, just to see the place and what it's like.

Ian: Our friend Richard had connections with the production company who make the BBC series and he showed them the pictures of me and Janette surfing in Australia, which had been used by Matt in The Scottish Sun. Richard said everyone's faces in the room immediately lit up. Not only were the pictures excellent, but apparently it showed we were still up for 'having fun' which is what they were after.

Janette: So at the start of November 2017 we arrived at Heathrow airport to discover who we would be spending a month with in India.

Ian: There was Boris's dad Stanley Johnson, TV presenter Selina Scott, former EastEnders actor Peter Dean, ex-jockey Bob Champion, and the actresses Susan George and Stephanie Beacham. But the person I was most pleased to see was Syd

Little from Little & Large. It's always good to meet someone you know.

Janette: We arrived in Rajasthan, in the north western region of India. On the way from the airport to our hotel we drove past this huge dance festival and I asked them to stop the car. As soon as she got out all the kids flocked around me, they were fascinated by this wee Scottish woman who was the same size as them. I was dancing with the children for ages. Then they all followed me down the road to my hotel - I was like the Pied Piper.

We also visited a school which was run by a charity for children of poor families. They showed us around the classrooms and the minute you walked in all the pupils stood to attention and were deathly silent. The walls had paint flaking off them, but the kids were all immaculate in their school uniforms with their books at the ready.

Ian: The poverty was incredible. But it's the opposites that bug you the most. We'd also been guests at the palace of Arvind Singh Mewar, the Maharana of Udaipur, then who have folk living in dirt.There doesn't seem to be much in-between. But we got on well with everyone on the show.

Janette: They were all good fun, although I think Stephanie thought I was hogging the camera a bit too much as she said to me 'Why do you always stand at the front of the pictures'. I told her, 'Well, I can hardly stand at the back, can I?'

Ian: In fact the only bust-up was when we took an overnight train journey to the Rajasthan capital Jaipur when a fight between two passengers broke out right outside Janette's bunk.

Janette: It was at two in the morning and I was sleeping in my bunk that just had the curtains separating us all when this fight woke me up. These two Indians guys were shouting and battering lumps out of each other right beside my head. I had taken a sleeping tablet so I didn't even know where I was, never mind what was going on.

Ian: After it all calmed down, about half a dozen Indians came up to apologise to us. They kept saying 'We're so, sorry, this is not how we normally behave'.

On another train we found an empty carriage and I said 'We'll all get in here' but when we looked up there was a guy sitting in the luggage rack. He didn't seem to bother sitting up there at all so we just left him to it.

Janette: That train had gaffer tape holding the windows in. It was in some state - I will never complain about British Rail again.

Ian: But Stanley Johnson was hilariously out of touch as you'd expect. He said to us 'You're very funny you two, what university did you study comedy at?' I think he thought we'd come through something like Footlights at Cambridge. I told him 'We never went to university – I left school at 14 and got a job in a store at the shipyards.

Stanley looked aghast and asked, 'Good God – what did your father say?' I said, 'He's the one who got me the job.' Stanley also cheekily signed up for ITV's I'm A Celebrity...Get Me Out Of Here before the third series of Marigold would have even aired. We all signed contracts saying that we weren't allowed to appear on any other reality show for 12 months. But Stanley obviously just ignored that bit. Rule breaking must run in the family. But he also refused to discuss politics with any of us. He was in contact with Boris every night as his son was having a bit of trouble back home as usual, but he was more interested in discussing our lives.

Janette: Stanley honestly didn't realise you had to start at the bottom in showbiz and climb the ladder. I think he thought it was all down to education.

Ian: When it finally aired in 2018 we couldn't believe the reaction. The series peaked with 5.4million viewers on BBC1 beating the Love Island finale of 4million.

I'm pretty sure it must have got more than that because

there wasn't a place we went where people didn't mention the series to us. It seemed to have gone down really well with us just being ourselves and not putting on an act for once.

Janette: It was also narrated by the actor Tom Hollander and viewers really seemed to like how he always referred to us as 'The Krankies' instead of Ian and Janette. I enjoyed all of it.

Ian: Well, apart from when a doctor wanted to stick a tube up her arse to help her bad back.

Janette: Because Bob Champion and I both have bad backs, the show's producers decided to send us to this Indian doctor to see what he could do. I went in first and he asked me all about my problems and I told him I had osteoporosis. He examined my back and said 'I can give you some medication that can help, but first of all I will give you an enema.'

I thought he was joking as the cameraman was sitting right across from us, but he was deadly serious. So I told him, 'I don't think so', but I should have said, 'You've got the wrong show — this isn't Embarrassing Bodies.'

Ian: I liked cooking curries with Syd. Matt told us people online were demanding a Syd Little and Ian Krankie cookery show. Syd is such a nice man and it was really good getting to know him again after all these years.

Janette: A year after India we got to film the spin-off series Marigold On Tour the following year. But instead of India, it was Mexico this time.

Ian: This time we were with Just Good Friends actor Paul Nicholas and TV chef Rosemary Shrager. We flew straight into Mexico's second-largest city, Guadalajara. When I knew where we were going I quickly Googled it and the first thing that came up was its crime rate. There had been 33,000 murders in that year alone. In fact there were so many murders the morgues were full to capacity forcing them to store bodies in a disused trailer park. And apparently the trailer parks weren't refrigerated, so you can imagine the smell.

The US State department had even issued a travel ban for its citizens saying the city has a 'high-threat' of murders and kidnapping. I thought 'That's all I need — Wee Jimmy to be kidnapped.'

Janette: I wasn't impressed by the city, although all the people we met were lovely.

Ian: There wasn't the same crippling poverty as we saw in India. The funny thing was that although Donald Trump was always banging on about all the Mexicans trying to get into The States, Mexico is actually full of Americans.

Janette: In our hotel they had all these masks hanging on all the walls from their Day Of The Dead festival. I'm just glad they didn't have any in the bedroom or I wouldn't have been able to get to sleep.

Ian: We also had to go into a native tribe hut as part of a spiritual enlightenment purification ceremony. They basically heated stones then poured water on them like they do in a sauna. You had to open your inner-self and all that, but actually what it did was help clear my chest. So it worked in some way I guess.

Janette: Rosemary did it too but went a funny colour in the tent. We also went to a Botox party. I only had one injection. It's not something I've ever gone in for before. But I didn't notice any difference.

Ian: While they were doing that, Paul and I had to stage a show in front of all these expat Americans, Canadians and Brits. He was really nervous because he's an actor rather than a comic so I wrote our script, but he kept asking 'Are you sure this is funny?' Then he asks me, 'Do you think we will get laughs?'. I said 'Of course we will,' and he replied, 'Well if we don't, I'm going to kick you in the bollocks.' We ended up doing a Donald Trump joke, with an immigration officer asking us loads of questions which the audience applauded. To be honest I didn't know how that would go down with the American exPats, but this lot weren't Trump fans.

Afterwards Paul was like 'That went rather well, we should get together back home and do some more'. So he went from a kick in the bollocks to wanting to form a new double act in the space of half an hour.

49

THE FINAL CURTAIN

Janette: At the end of our panto run in 2018 we were approached by London's Victoria and Albert Museum who asked if they could put Wee Jimmy Krankie's red schoolboy hat on display.

Ian: It was for an exhibition of comedians and their iconic props and the cap would be included along with Tommy Cooper's Fez and the glasses worn by Eric Morecambe and Dame Edna Everage, Ken Dodd's tickling stick and Charlie Chaplain's walking stick. So Jimmy was in very illustrious company.

Janette: The cap, and Jimmy's entire uniform had been almost everywhere with me since we cobbled it together in 1970. We were just about to go to Australia for our three month stay and for the first time I felt happy to let it go. In fact, it was more than that - I would have gladly given the V&A the whole outfit to keep forever.

Ian: We would always start planning the next season's panto from the summertime onwards, working out what new songs and comedy we're going to do. But for the last couple of years it was really starting to make Janette anxious. She began to resent the whole process even though it's what we'd been doing for years.

Janette: I'd had enough. I'd worked long enough. I didn't want the hassle any more. The worry of thinking what we'd do next and then rehearsing the lyrics or the words over and over again.

Ian: Then there was the osteoporosis in Janette's back, which had been getting worse since she was first diagnosed with it in 2017. Her Harley Street specialist had told us to take it easy on stage but we didn't even mention to him that we were still doing the ventriloquist act, where I threw Janette about all over the place.

Janette: My consultant hadn't even been happy when he saw me doing yoga on The Real Marigold Hotel. He told me I had to be 'Very, very careful' doing any movements like that.

Ian: It got us thinking that we had been taking too big a risk with Janette's health by continuing to perform live.

Janette: So in June 2019, shortly after we returned to Torquay from Australia, we decided to call it a day.

Ian: That meant our last ever live show had been on December 30, 2018, at the SEC in Glasgow. We just didn't know it was our last show at the time.

Janette: We would have liked to have finished our panto career at the London Palladium because that is where it all started for us with the Royal Variety Performance in 1978.

Ian: We told Qdos we wanted to play there, not at the top of the bill, but just to bow out at the Palladium. But they had already cast the panto for that year and that was that.

Janette: We were still doing occasional TV slots and appeared on Harry Hill's Alien Fun Capsule that month, but as far as performing live shows was concerned that is now a thing of the past for us. While I was ready to call it quits, I don't think Ian was.

Ian: I would have been happy to continue but I didn't like the way the build-up to the shows was making Janette feel. I wasn't worried about money as we hadn't even started taking our own private pensions yet and had been getting our state pension for years.

Janette: Or my Donna Karan fund as I like to call it.

Ian: But I did like the whole social side of pantos. Meeting up with John Barrowman every year, spending Christmas Day with the cast who were too far from home to travel back for the day. Getting pissed in the pub. I loved all that.

Janette: I did too but there were things I wouldn't miss like having to do promo for the panto, although the photocalls with John were always a riot. And then there were the promotions we did with Matt for The Scottish Sun.

Author's note Matt: I will never forget the day my then editor Alan Muir shouted across to me 'Do you think The Krankies would dress up as Santa and his elf and we could give them away to readers as a prize?' I said 'Let me check.' I put my request to Ian and Janette on the phone and they said 'Yes' on the spot. The competition was puffed on our front page where we asked readers to come up with a reason why they wanted to win The Krankies, whether it was to entertain an old folks' home or cheer up someone in need of a laugh. It was one of the biggest competitions we've run in years with thousands of entries.

Ian: We were driven around the Central Belt of Scotland to meet six different Scottish Sun readers and their families. But on the last visit there was a dead body...

Janette: The last competition winner we were visiting that day had been a young woman who had said she needed cheering up after losing her gran. Apparently her gran used to take her to see us in panto every year.

Ian: Although we had no idea just how recently bereaved she was until we turned up at her house as Santa and his Elf and walked right into the middle of a wake.

Janette: This young woman's gran was still in the spare room in her coffin. She asked if we would like to see her and pay our respects but I didn't think it appropriate to do so dressed as an elf. I also had bells on my hat and shoes and every time I moved it sounded like Jingle Bells.

Ian: It was also quite a rough household with some of the mourners appearing to have been drowning their sorrows with more than just booze.

Janette: One of the men just kept staring at me without saying a word.

Ian: He had a confused look on his face, although I like to think at whatever time he came round the next day, he'd say to himself 'I had one fucking weird trip last night - The Krankies came to see me dressed as Santa and his elf.'

Janette: So we would miss all that, but not enough to want to carry on.

50

EPILOGUE

Janette: Well this has pretty much been our whole life story so far. I hope you've enjoyed the book as much as I've enjoyed what has been a brilliant life. It's funny though because I've met people who think Ian and I haven't had a life at all, because we never started a family and lived like nomads, constantly moving about, moving houses, living out of suitcases. Someone once said that we had a 'funny way of life' and we thought that'd make a great title of a book one day. But it has been a funny way of life because we have had so many laughs.

Ian: I don't remember a day that's gone past where we haven't laughed. How many couples can say that? Even when Janette's mum was ill, we'd still break the tension at some point of the day by having a chuckle, because that's just the way we are.

Janette: Of course we've had fights, but we've only fallen out for a day at the most. Ian and I never hold grudges, especially against each other. We talk about things if there's something annoying us, which people from our generation tend not to do. They'd rather just go in a huff and not speak, but what does that solve?

Ian: If we're angry we'll have a right good swear at each other - call each other all the bastards of the world. You'd be surprised how calm you feel afterwards.

Janette: But after that we'll then listen to each other - and I mean listen, not shouting over the top of what we're trying to say, and then talk about it. But what I can't believe is that since meeting Ian when I was 19, all those years have passed so quickly.

Ian: I would say we've had a lucky life. To be able to do what we have, we've been the luckiest people in the world. In 1977 Janette and I were in a swimming pool in Jersey at three in the morning with four of our dancers all drinking Champagne, having a barbecue overlooking a beautiful bay. And we weren't even famous at that point. I remember saying to Janette 'This really is the life - I wonder what'll be like if we ever get famous and successful?' The thing is it never got any better than that, but it was always that good.

Janette: We really have lived the high-life and I don't mean a pretentious social climbing high-life, we were never into that. I just mean we mixed with some fantastic people and did some fantastic things that we simply wouldn't have done if I'd stuck to my office job back in Glasgow all those years before.

Ian: To be honest when we did become famous, it was really just a hindrance as it restricts the fun you can have - in case we got caught! Nowadays it appears that people just want fame and money. They don't want to even work for it, they just want to turn up for a few auditions then end up on a Saturday night TV show then go to number one, all in the space of a few weeks. We had to serve an apprenticeship if you like, working for years and years around the clubs, making our mistakes and learning from them. Not making our mistakes in front of millions of TV viewers.

But our manager Stan Dallas once said to us that if someone has been in the business for 35 years then they have to be good as there's no way they can con the public and the promoters for that length of time. If they were crap they would have been out of the business 30 years ago. Well, we ended up working far longer than that and I'd like to think that the people who came to see us left thinking the same. That we were actually pretty good. That we made them laugh.

Janette: I also think the secret to our long marriage is I do what I like and he does what he's told!

Ian: I'd also say that two TVs are essential. Seriously, I have my own in my room to watch things I like on Netflix.

Janette: And I love my quiz shows like Pointless. So at least with two TVs you're not arguing over the remote control.

But we've been very, very lucky in life. God's been good to us. I just hope we can stay happy and healthy for years to come.

The End

AFTERWORD
THE GHOSTWRITER'S STORY - BY MATT BENDORIS

It was at a sell-out performance of Dick Whittington at the Birmingham Hippodrome when Janette walked on stage dressed as Brummie legend Ozzy Osbourne, bleeping out her curses with a hand held electronic clicker before she 'accidentally' missed one of the F-bombs. That's when the bloke sitting directly in front of me lost all control. Grabbing his backside he awkwardly shuffled towards the nearest loo - the stench was overpowering.

Afterwards, when I told Ian about the theatre goer's messy misfortune, he was as quick witted as ever, saying 'We should put that on the posters "So funny you'll shit yourself".'

What was remarkable was at that point Ian and Janette were just a few months shy of their 70th birthdays, yet they were still packing in sell-out crowds and having them rolling - and a lot worse - in the aisles.

At the stage door afterwards, a 50-strong queue waited patiently for autographs and selfies long after the final curtain.

And that's the amazing thing about The Krankies, they may have been a 'Scottish act' but they were household names across the entire UK for decades.

I first met the duo in 1999 a few years after they had returned to Glasgow's Pavilion Theatre, where a 16-year-old Janette Anderson performed in her first festive show, Jack Milroy's World Of Widow Krankie, in 1963.

The pair would admit themselves that their careers were on the slide. If showbiz is a rollercoaster then they had peaked during the 80s heyday of Crackerjack! and The Krankies Elektronik Komik, and now had hit the troughs working the cruise ship circuit.

And so it was that our first meeting was when their ship docked at Palma, Majorca, where the Pavilion Theatre's indomitable manager Iain Gordon had spared all expense sending me - the hotel room in Magaluf, complete with fag butts under the bed, remains an all-time low for me accommodation-wise. Knowing Iain Gordon the way I do, he probably arranged that on purpose.

But the Pavilion had paid my fare as a feature writer from The Scottish Sun because they were trying to drum up interest in The Krankies, who were their top of the bill act that year, but getting zero interest from the rest of the press.

I think it's fair to say that it was love at first sight with Ian and Janette, well it certainly was for me. Like many my age (I was born in 1970), I grew up with them, becoming besotted the moment I first saw them on Crackerjack!. Of course I was then left distraught when some smart arse in school explained that he was a she and what's worse, she was married to him!

But on finally meeting them, what I loved the most was they may have been in their early 50s, but were still up for a laugh. Ian had arranged for the ship's photographer to do a Titanic-style photo shoot at the bow of the ship, then they larked about on the bridge with the captain's wheel. They were hilarious and so were the photos. Afterwards Ian and Janette asked if I would like to join them for a meal, along with half a dozen of the crew, but not before we'd been to the supermarket to stock up on their supplies of red wine.

I have never hit it off so instantly with anyone else in this business they call show. There was I, getting a crash course in the best of reds (they like them light, French and expensive) while Janette pushed the shopping trolley around practically looking through the cart's metal grill.

Now that is something I have never gotten used to - just how petite Janette is. Every time I meet her it always takes me that second or two to remember her teensy weensy stature.

After a fabulous meal I departed back to the vomit filled streets of Magaluf while they returned to their cabin, and that was basically it. I periodically stayed in touch, then in 2003 I heard them both on BBC Radio Scotland's satirical football show Off The Ball. They immediately explained to the hosts Tam Cowan and Stuart Cosgrove that they knew nothing about football, but proceeded to tell stories about their incredible career, including the Roger De Courcey tale. That got me thinking, if that was just one story from their decades in the business, how many others would they have? Enough to fill a book? Well, it turns out they did - this one.

It took me a year to write - it was my first book - and I'd talk to them early in the morning (my time) and late in the evening (their time) in Australia, charting their careers and also trying to get the word count up to the 70,000 count the London publisher was demanding.

Then when they returned to Glasgow for panto, I'd get pissed on red wine with them at their rented apartment on their Mondays off.

And it's true what Ian says in the footnote of the infamous Ding Dong chapter, that their autobiography hardly caused any ripples, never mind waves when it first came out, however it did begin to garner them a cult following. I would get texts from friends saying 'Jimmy Carr has just said on 8 Out of 10 Cat that

The Krankies is the best celebrity autobiography he's ever read.' There was no punchline. It had just been a statement of fact. Then before Jonathan Ross's BBC career went tits up over Sachsgate, I heard him say something very similar on Radio 2, demanding on air that his producer line up Ian and Janette for next weekend's show.

But then, just shortly after it was published in September 2004, Janette fell from a beanstalk.

I was in the newsroom of The Scottish Sun when it happened and immediately all eyes were on me to deliver as the official Krankies biographer. There was much mirth around the place about the accident - it was after all a Krankie falling off a beanstalk - but the seriousness of the situation hit me hard when I called Ian who was still in floods of tears, with panic rising in his voice he told me how he had 'Heard a crack' and then the mechanical beanstalk had collapsed with Janette falling 20ft onto the stage. He just kept repeating over and over again how he should have never let Janette on that 'bloody beanstalk'.

I raced to Glasgow's Royal Infirmary where news of the accident was being reported on BBC Radio One, again almost with an air of joviality over the bizarreness of it all.

At the hospital, Ian was too distraught to leave Janette's bedside and asked their pal Jim Higgins to face the press. By this point the accident was on all the evening news channels. Again I doubt it would have been reported this widely had a beanstalk not been involved.

Jonathan Ross even did an opening quip about it on his BBC chat show just days later, saying how the ambulance crew didn't know whether to take Janette to the 'Geratric ward or the children's hospital.' It was a good line, but perhaps a little too soon as it was still no laughing matter for Ian or poor Janette.

In the days afterwards I was professionally obliged to get a picture of Janette recovering in hospital. I hated having to ask but the best way was just to come right out with it. Ian quite understandably said no as Janette was still sore and badly bruised. He didn't want everyone to see her like that, but he did invite me to visit her after she had been moved to a private hospital in Glasgow's West End.

Oh, what a sight. She really was in a sorry state. Her little black and blue body barely making a bump in the white starched sheets that covered her. She cried as she took my hand and then told me to thank all the wellwishers who had written to her, which I duly did in the following day's newspaper. That was one of the times that my personal and professional life clashed, but Ian and Janette promised there and then that I would get the first proper interview - and pictures - when she had fully recovered. She wanted to be photographed looking her best, not like a 'broken doll' as Ian described her.

And she was back to her best just two months later when I met them at Heathrow airport mid-February 2005 before they flew to Oz to recuperate. Then when she returned to the stage for the first time since the fall later that summer, I was there again in Blackpool to cover it. That was a great trip. Before the show I had been walking along the North Pier chatting to Janette, when this huge Lancashire man coming towards us without warning grabbed her by the shoulder and said 'What was it you had again luv? Was it cancer?' Janette politely replied 'No, I fell off a beanstalk.' The man turned to his tiny wife and said 'I knew it was something' and walked off quite satisfied. But Ian and Janette have been used to these encounters, or being recognised, ever since that breakthrough performance at the Royal Variety Show in 1978, when their lives changed forever.

And as always with Ian and Janette, they knew the best restaurants and the best nightlife to go to afterwards, taking me to Funny Girls, where the drag acts were beside themselves with excitement that The Krankies were there to see them.

Although everyone seems to think TV is the be all and end all (if you're not on it, you want to be on it) I never found that to be the case with Ian and Janette. They always saw panto as their bread and butter.

They made a triumphant return to their home city Glasgow with John Barrowman in Aladdin in 2010 which had all the production values of a major west end show - including 3D effects - rather than a panto.

I will never forgot the glee of watching my own son and daughter Andrew and Brooke, then just seven and four, howl with laughter at The Krankies along with my wife Amanda, my mum Annie and my dear Aunt Sam - three generations of family - enchanted by them the way I had been all those years ago watching Crackerjack!. Afterwards one of my kid's excitable cousins said to Janette 'You're the funniest person on the planet' From the mouths of babes huh?

One of the best weeks I spent with Ian and Janette was when I was dispatched to Australia in March 2017 to interview them ahead of their landmark 70th birthdays. Qantas sponsored my trip, which meant I flew Business Class all the way there and back - what's not to like? I also had a penthouse apartment overlooking their favourite spot on Kalgoorlie beach where we did hilarious pictures of them on a surfboard with Janette in a wetsuit as Wee Jimmy. We then did a shoot with a kangaroo (of course), on a golf course and in front of the Sydney Opera House.

Apparently these pics proved instrumental in them being offered the only TV show they wanted to be a part of - The Real Marigold Hotel on the BBC. So later that year they left for India where they would be followed by cameras for a month. The show proved to be a pivotal moment for Janette who was seen as herself for the first time and not just a cheeky schoolboy. And the public liked what they saw, especially when she broke down in tears talking about her marriage to Ian, ahead of their

Golden Wedding Anniversary in October 2019. When they returned home they were continually being stopped in the street by fans of the show. But that was also when Janette decided to bring the curtain down on a career of live performances which had started for her at the age of 16. By then she was in her 70s and had simply had enough.

Janette once told me 'I'd have retired years ago if it hadn't been for you' which I take as a huge compliment. If I had anything to do with extending their careers for new generations of kids and families to enjoy, then I make absolutely no apology.

Janette was desperate to quit performing but she feared Ian would miss it, as panto wasn't just a job to them, it was a social structure. Past cast members and dancers and crew stayed in touch with The Krankies for decades after working with them because of the Christmas Days they spent together, with Ian cooking for everyone, or the laughs they had on the road. So watching that final panto run in December 2018 with my aunt Sam now painfully thin and just weeks left to live (she would pass away on January 2nd, 2019) I knew it truly was the end of an era.

Ian is perhaps the sharpest and funniest person I have ever known - Janette once said to me 'There is no one quicker'. I can talk to him about anything from politics to the best shows on Netflix, but even with all that talent he knew he didn't stand a chance standing next to Janette, as all eyes would always be on her.

And that's the thing about Janette - she may be the smallest woman I have ever met but she had the natural ability to fill even the biggest of stages.

Printed in Great Britain
by Amazon